Dr Melanie Fennell is an internationally recognized cognitive therapy practitioner and trainer. She is Director of an Advanced Cognitive Therapy course based at Oxford Cognitive Therapy Centre and Oxford University. She is a recognized expert in low self-esteem and has run workshops and presented papers at major international conferences.

The Overcoming series was initiated by Peter Cooper, Professor of Psychology at the University of Reading and Honorary NHS Consultant Clinical Psychologist. His original book on bulimia nervosa and binge-eating founded the series in 1993 and continues to help many thousands of people in the USA, the UK and Europe. The aim of the series is to help people with a wide range of common problems and disorders to take control of their own recovery programme using the latest techniques of cognitive behavioural therapy. Each book, with its specially tailored programme, is devised by a practising clinician. Many books in the Overcoming series are now recommended by the UK Department of Health under the Books on Prescription scheme.

Other titles in the Overcoming series:

3-part self-help courses

Overcoming Anxiety Self-Help Course
Overcoming Bulimia Nervosa and Binge-Eating Self-Help Course

Single volume books

Overcoming Anger and Irritability
Overcoming Anorexia Nervosa
Overcoming Anxiety
Bulimia Nervosa and Binge-Eating
Overcoming Childhood Trauma
Overcoming Chronic Fatigue
Overcoming Chronic Pain
Overcoming Compulsive Gambling
Overcoming Depression
Overcoming Insomnia and Sleep Problems
Overcoming Low Self-Esteem
Overcoming Mood Swings
Overcoming Obsessive Compulsive Disorder
Overcoming Panic
Overcoming Relationship Problems
Overcoming Sexual Problems
Overcoming Social Anxiety and Shyness
Overcoming Traumatic Stress
Overcoming Weight Problems
Overcoming Your Smoking Habit

All titles in this series are available by mail order.
Please see the order form at the back of this workbook.

www.overcoming.co.uk

OVERCOMING
LOW SELF-ESTEEM
SELF-HELP COURSE

A 3-part programme based on
Cognitive Behavioural Techniques

Part Three: Changing the Rules, Creating a New Bottom Line, and Looking to the Future

Melanie Fennell

ROBINSON

ROBINSON

First published in Great Britain in 2006 by Robinson

Copyright © Melanie Fennell, 2006

9 10

A CIP catalogue record for this book
is available from the British Library.

Important Note
This book is not intended as a substitute for medical advice or treatment.
Any person with a condition requiring medical attention should consult
a qualified medical practitioner or suitable therapist.

ISBN: 978-1-84529-237-9 (3-part pack)
ISBN: 978-1-84529-392-5 (Part One)
ISBN: 978-1-84529-393-2 (Part Two)
ISBN: 978-1-84529-394-9 (Part Three)

Printed and bound in Great Britain by Ashford Colour Press

Robinson
An imprint of
Little, Brown Book Group
Carmelite House
50 Victoria Embankment
London EC4Y 0DZ

An Hachette UK Company

www.hachette.co.uk
www.littlebrown.co.uk

Contents

Introduction: How to Use this Workbook

This is a self-help course for dealing with low self-esteem. It has two aims:

1 To help you develop a better understanding of the problem

2 To teach you the practical skills you will need in order to change

How the course works

The *Overcoming Low Self-Esteem Self-Help Course* will help you understand how low self-esteem develops and what keeps it going, and then to make changes in your life so that you begin to feel more confident and more kindly and accepting towards yourself.

These books are designed to help you work, either by yourself or with your healthcare practitioner, to overcome low self-esteem. With plenty of questionnaires, charts, worksheets and practical exercises, the three parts together make up a structured course.

Part One explained:

● What low self-esteem is

● How low self-esteem affects people

● How negative experiences affect people

● What keeps low self-esteem going

Part Two explained:

● How to recognize and deal with anxious predictions

● How to recognize and question self-critical thoughts

● How to identify your positive qualities

● How to gain a balanced view of yourself and start enjoying life

Part Three explains:

- What Rules for Living are

- How to change your Rules for Living

- How to recognize and change your central belief about yourself

- How to draft and fine-tune an Action Plan for the future

How long will the course take?

Each book will take at least two or three weeks to work through – but do not worry if you feel that you need to give each one extra time. Some things can be understood and changed quite quickly, but others take longer. You will know when you are ready to move on to the next workbook. Completing the entire course could take only two to three months, but this will depend on how quickly you wish to work. Take your time, and go at the pace that suits you best.

Getting the most from the course

Here are some tips to help you get the most from the workbooks:

- These workbooks are not priceless antiques – they are practical tools. So feel free not only to write on the worksheets and charts, but also to underline and high-light things, and to write comments and questions in the margins. By the time you have finished with a workbook, it should look well and truly used.

- You will also find lots of spaces in the main text. These are for you to write down your thoughts and ideas, and your responses to the questions.

- Keep an open mind and be willing to experiment with new ideas and skills. These books will sometimes ask you to think about painful issues. However, if low self-esteem is distressing you and restricting your life, it really is worth making the effort to overcome it. The rewards will be substantial.

- Be prepared to invest time in doing the practical exercises – set aside 20 to 30 minutes each day if you can.

- Try to answer all the questions and do the exercises, even if you have to come back to some of them later. There may be times when you get stuck and can't think how to take things forward. If this happens, don't get angry with yourself or give up. Just put the book aside and come back to it later, when you are feeling more relaxed.

- You may find it helpful to work through the books with a friend. Two heads are often better than one. And you may be able to encourage each other to persist, even when one of you is finding it hard.

- Use the Thoughts and Reflections section at the back of the book to write down anything you read that has been particularly helpful to you.

- Re-read the workbook. You may get more out of it once you've had a chance to think about some of the ideas and put them into practice for a little while.

- Each workbook builds on what has already been covered. So what you learn when working with one will help you when you come to the next. It's quite possible simply to dip into different ones as you please, but you may get most out of the series if you follow them through systematically, step by step.

A note of caution

These workbooks will not help everyone who has low self-esteem. If you find that focusing on self-esteem is actually making you feel worse instead of better, or if your negative beliefs about yourself are so strong that you cannot even begin to use the ideas and practical skills described, you may be suffering from clinical depression. The recognized signs of clinical depression include:

- Constantly feeling sad, down, depressed or empty

- General lack of interest in what's going on around you

- A big increase or decrease in your appetite and weight

- A marked change in your sleep patterns

- Noticeable speeding up or slowing down in your movements and how you go about things

- Feeling of being tired and low in energy

- An intense sense of guilt or worthlessness

- Difficulty in concentrating and making decisions

- A desire to hurt yourself or a feeling that you might be better off dead

If you have had five or more of these symptoms (including low mood or loss of interest) for two weeks or more, you should seek professional help from a doctor, counsellor or psychotherapist. There is nothing shameful about seeking this sort of professional help – any more than there is anything shameful about taking your car to a garage if it is not working as it should, or going to see a lawyer if you have legal problems. It simply means taking your journey towards self-knowledge and self-acceptance with the help of a friendly guide, rather than striking out alone.

SECTION 1: Changing the Rules

In Part Two, Section 3, you focused on acknowledging and appreciating your good points and positive qualities, and on making the most of everyday pleasures and achievements. Now we shall begin work on an important barrier to self-acceptance: rigid, demanding Rules for Living. These may have been formed many years ago, and are designed to help you get by in the world, assuming your Bottom Line (negative belief about yourself) to be true. In reality, they place heavy demands on you and restrict your life.

This section will help you to understand:

- where Rules for Living come from

- how to recognize Rules for Living

- how to identify your own Rules for Living

- how Rules for Living affect your daily life

- how to find new Rules for Living

- how to act on them

When you have low self-esteem, your Rules for Living determine the standards you expect of yourself, what you should do in order to be loved and accepted, and how you should behave in order to feel that you are a good and worthwhile person. Personal rules demand that you 'keep to the straight and narrow' and give little room for manoeuvre. They often include a statement of what the consequences will be, if you fail to meet their terms. For instance, someone whose Bottom Line was 'I am unlovable' might have a Rule for Living that says: 'If I allow people to see my true self, they will reject me.'

Since the consequences of breaking such rules are generally painful, you may have become very sensitive to situations where you are in danger of not meeting their terms. These are the situations that are likely to activate your Bottom Line, leading to the vicious circle of anxious predictions and self-critical thinking described in Part One, Section 3. The flowchart that follows is a reminder of how this happens.

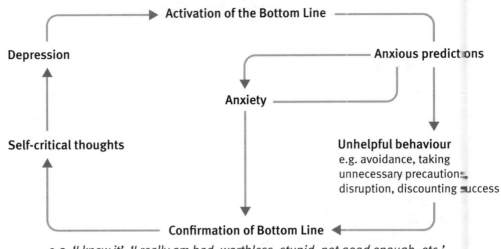

e.g. 'I knew it', 'I really am bad, worthless, stupid, not good enough, etc.'

As you work through this section, it is worth summarizing in writing what you discover about each of your Rules, your line of argument when you question it, your new Rule and your Action Plan for putting it into practice. You will find questions in this section, with spaces for you to write, and a summary worksheet on pp. 40–2. These are designed to help you to organize your thoughts. This is important because unhelpful Rules for Living can be difficult to change. Writing your ideas down as you go along will help you to keep your new perspective in view and make it easier for you to act on it, even when the going gets tough.

Where do Rules for Living come from?

Rules can be helpful. They enable us to make sense of what happens to us, to recognize repeating patterns, and to respond to new experiences without bewilderment. They can even help us to survive (e.g. 'I must always look both ways before crossing the road').

Parents pass on rules to their children, so that they will be able to deal with life independently (e.g. 'Make sure you eat a balanced diet'). Children also absorb rules from their families purely by observation. They notice connections (e.g. 'If I don't tidy my room, Mum will do it for me') and these can become a basis for more general rules (e.g. 'If things go wrong, someone will be there to pick up the pieces'). They notice what is praised and what is criticized, what brings a smile to a parent's face and what causes a frown. All these experiences can become a basis for personal rules with a lasting impact on how people live their lives.

However, some rules, instead of helping us to make sense of the world, trap us in unhelpful patterns and prevent us from achieving our life goals. They place demands on us that are impossible to meet, and make no concessions to circumstances or individual needs (e.g. 'You must always give 110 per cent, no matter what the cost to yourself'). These extreme and unbending rules create problems. They become a straitjacket, restricting freedom of movement and preventing change.

Rules that make you vulnerable to low self-esteem may determine the performance you expect of yourself in a range of different situations. Let's take Jesse, from Workbook 1, as an example. Here's a reminder of his case study:

CASE STUDY: Jesse

Jesse's father was an insurance salesman. He had never realized his ambitions to rise to a manager's position, and put this down to the fact that his parents had failed to support him during his years at school. They had never seemed particularly interested in what he was doing, and it was easy to skip school and neglect his homework. He was determined not to make the same mistake with his own children. Every day, at the supper table, he would question them about what they had learned. Everyone had to have an answer, and the answer had to be good enough.

Jesse remembered dreading the sight of his father's car in the drive when he came home. It meant another grilling. He was sure his mind would go blank and he would be unable to think of anything to say. When this happened, his father's face would fall in disappointment. Jesse could see that he was letting his father down. He felt he fully deserved the close questioning that followed. 'If you can't do better than this,' his father would say, 'you'll never get anywhere in life.' In his heart of hearts, Jesse agreed. It was clear to him that he was not good enough: he would never make it.

Jesse's Bottom Line was 'I am not good enough' and his main Rule for Living was 'Unless I always get it right, I will never get anywhere in life'. This type of perfectionist rule may not only require high-quality performance in the work environment, but might also require perfection in your physical appearance, in where you live or in how you carry out the most ordinary of everyday activities.

Rules can restrict your freedom to be your true self with other people. They may make you feel that approval, liking, love and intimacy are all dependent on your acting (or being) a certain way. Rules may even influence how you react to your own feelings and thoughts. For instance, you may base your good opinion of yourself on being fully in control of your emotions. But unhelpful rules like these imprison you. They build a wall of expectations and demands around you. This is your chance to break out.

Rules for Living and the Bottom Line

The heart of low self-esteem is the belief that your Bottom Line is true. Rules for Living provide you with 'escape clauses', ways to get round the Bottom Line. For example, at heart, you might believe yourself to be incompetent. But *so long as* you work very hard all the time and set yourself high standards, you can override your incompetence and feel OK about yourself. Or you might believe yourself to be unattractive. But *so long as* you are the life and soul of the party, maybe no one will notice and so again you can feel OK about yourself.

Rules like these can work very well, much of the time. For long periods, you may be able to maintain your good opinion of yourself by obeying them. But there is a fundamental problem. Such rules allow you to wallpaper over what you feel to be the real truth about yourself (your Bottom Line). But they do not change it. Indeed, the more successful they are, and the better you are at meeting their demands, the less opportunity they give you to stand back, question your Bottom Line, and accept yourself as you are. So the Bottom Line stays there, waiting to be wheeled into place whenever your rules are in danger of being broken. On the opposite page you can see how this worked for Jesse.

How can you recognize Rules for Living?

Rules are learned

Unhelpful rules are rarely formally taught, but tend to be absorbed through experience and observation. This is rather like a child learning to speak without learning the formal rules of grammar. Personal Rules for Living are often the same – you may consistently act in accordance with them, without having ever expressed them in so many words. This is probably because they reflect decisions you made about how to operate in the world, when you were very young. Your rules probably made perfect sense when you drew them up, but they were based on the limited experience available to you at the time, and so may be out of date and irrelevant to your life now.

Rules are part of the culture we grow up in

Our social and family heritage is comprised of rules. For example, society has evolved certain rules about how men and women should act. We absorb these ideas from our earliest years and, even if we disagree with them, it may be difficult to act

Jesse's Rules for Living and his Bottom Line

Bottom Line

I am not good enough.

↓

Rules for Living

Unless I get it right, I will never get anywhere in life.

If someone criticizes me, it means I have failed.

↓

Policy

Go for perfection every time.

Do everything you can to avoid criticism.

↓

Advantage

I do a lot of really good work and get good feedback for it.

BUT: Problem

At heart, I still believe my Bottom Line 100 per cent.

Obeying the rules keeps it quiet, but it doesn't go away.

Plus:

However hard I try, it's not possible to be perfect and avoid criticism
all the time.

So:

The more I succeed, the more anxious I get.

I feel a fraud – any minute now, I'm going to fall off the tightrope.

And whenever something goes wrong, or someone is less than
wholly positive about me, I feel terrible – straight back to the Bottom Line.

against them. We may be punished for attempting to do so by social disapproval. The difficulties women still have in progressing in the workplace, and the struggle to establish a meaningful role for men in childcare, would be examples of this.

Personal rules are often like exaggerated versions of the rules of the society we grew up in. Western society, for example, places a high value on independence and achievement. In a particular individual, these social pressures might be expressed through rules like 'I must never ask for help' or 'If I'm not on top, I'm a flop'. However, social and cultural rules can change, and such changes (via the family) will have an impact on personal rules. In England, for example, the 'stiff upper lip' used to be highly valued. In the individual, this might be expressed as: 'If I show my feelings, people will write me off as a wimp'. More recently, however, there has been more emphasis on the importance of openly expressing vulnerability and emotion. In the individual, this might become: 'If I do not lay all my feelings on the table, it means I am hard and inhuman.' Whatever your background, the chances are that your personal rules reflect the culture you grew up in, as well as that of your immediate family.

Your rules are unique to you

Although your rules may have much in common with those of other people growing up in the same culture, no one else will exactly share your experiences of life. Even within the same family, each child's experience is different. However much parents try to be fair to their children, each one will be treated a little differently, loved in a different way. So your rules are unique.

Rules are rigid and resist change

Rules are rigid because they shape how you see things and how you interpret what happens to you on a day-to-day basis (see Part One, Section 3). Negative biases in perception and in interpretation reinforce and strengthen them. Rules encourage you to behave in ways that make it difficult for you to discover just how unhelpful they are. So Jesse, for example, not only strives to be '100 per cent great' when completing a particularly important assignment at work, but also has perfectionist standards for everything he does. This means that he has no opportunity to discover that, given his natural talents and skills, he has no real need to place such pressure on himself.

Rules are linked to powerful emotions

Strong emotions are a sign that you have broken the rules, or that you are at risk of doing so. You react with fear, not concern. You feel depressed or despairing, not sad. You experience rage, not irritation. These powerful emotions tell you that a rule is in operation, and that the Bottom Line is gearing up for activation. In this sense, they are useful clues. However, their strength may also make it difficult to observe what is going on from a detached perspective.

Rules are unreasonable

Like anxious predictions and self-critical thoughts, personal Rules for Living do not match the facts. They do not fit the way the world works, or what can reasonably be expected of the average human being. Jesse (p. 5) recognizes this point when he acknowledges that it is not always possible to be perfect or to avoid criticism. We shall return to this point in more detail when we come to reformulate your personal rules.

Rules are extreme

Unhelpful rules are over-generalizations. They do not recognize that what is helpful changes according to the circumstances in which you find yourself. They do not respond to variations in time and place, or recognize that what works at one time of your life will not work at another. This is reflected in their language: 'always'/'never', 'everyone'/'no one', 'everything'/'nothing'. They prevent you from selecting the best course of action, flexibly responding according to your particular needs at a particular moment in time.

Rules are absolute; they do not allow for shades of grey. This may be because they were developed when you were very young, before you had the breadth of experience to see things from a more complex perspective.

Rules are based on things that cannot be guaranteed

The sequence Jesse identified on p. 5 illustrates an important point. He noticed that his rules required something that was in fact impossible: unfailing 100 per cent performance and never encountering criticism of any kind. This is characteristic of unhelpful rules linked to low self-esteem. They mean that your sense of your own worth is dependent on things that are impossible (e.g. being perfect, always being in full control of what happens to you), or outside your control (e.g. being accepted and liked by everyone).

People hang self-esteem on a whole range of pegs:

- Being young
- Being beautiful
- Being fit and healthy
- Being in paid employment
- Being a parent
- Having money
- Having social status
- Being at the right school or college
- Having a partner
- Being a particular weight or shape
- Being top dog
- Achieving success
- Being famous
- Being loved
- Having children who are doing well
- Being secure
- Being sexually attractive, and so on

The list is endless. But none of these things can be guaranteed. We all get old; we all get sick from time to time; we may be damaged or disabled; we may lose our employment; our children leave home (or if they don't, that becomes a cause of concern); there are times in our lives when we have no one special to love us or when our futures are insecure; and so on. All these things are fragile, and could be taken away. This means that, if we depend on them in order to feel good about ourselves, our self-esteem is also fragile. To be happy with yourself simply for existing, just as you are, regardless of your circumstances, puts you in a far stronger position.

How can you identify your own Rules for Living?

You are looking for general rules that reflect what you expect of yourself, your standards for how you should behave, your sense of what is acceptable and what is not allowed, and your idea of what is necessary in order to succeed in life and achieve satisfying relationships. In essence, you are defining what you have to do or be in order to feel good about yourself. If you have low self-esteem, the chances are that these standards are demanding and unrealistic (more, for example, than you would expect of any other person) and that, when you explore their impact, you will discover that they actually prevent you from having a secure sense of personal worth.

Rules for Living are usually expressed in one of three ways: assumptions, drivers and value judgements.

Assumptions

These are your ideas about the connections between self-esteem and other things in life. These usually take the form of 'If…, then…' statements. (They can also be phrased as 'Unless… , then…'.)

Here are some examples of assumptions:

- *If* I allow anyone to get close to me, *[then]* they will hurt and exploit me

- *If* someone criticizes me, *[then]* it means I have failed

- *Unless* I do everything people expect of me, *[then]* I will be rejected

- Nothing I do is worthwhile *unless* it is recognized by others (i.e. *Unless* what I do is recognized by others, *[then]* it is not worthwhile)

Assumptions like these are rather like anxious predictions. They describe what you think will happen if you act (or fail to act) in a certain way. This immediately provides a clue to one important way of changing them. They can be tested by setting up the 'If…' and seeing if the 'then…' really happens. As we learned with anxious predictions, the threat could be more apparent than real.

Drivers

These are the 'shoulds', 'musts' and 'oughts' that compel us to act in particular ways, or be particular kinds of people, in order to feel good about ourselves. Drivers usually link up with a hidden '*or else…*'. Here are some examples:

- I must never let anyone see my true self (*or else they will see what a bad person I am and reject me*)

- I must always keep myself under tight control (*or else I will go over the top and spoil things*)

- I should be able to cope with anything life throws at me (*or else I am weak*)

You can see from these examples that the '*or else…*' may be very close to the Bottom Line. In fact, the '*or else…*' may be a simple statement of the Bottom Line: '*or else… it means that I am inadequate/unlovable/incompetent/ugly*' or whatever.

Value judgements

These are statements about how it would be if you acted (or did not act) in a particular way, or if you were (or were not) a particular kind of person. In a sense, these are rather similar to assumptions, but their terms are less clear, and may need to be questioned in order to be fully understood. Examples would be: 'It's terrible to make mistakes', 'Being rejected is unbearable', 'It's crucial to be on top of things'. If you find rules that take this form, you need to ask yourself some questions in order to find out what exactly you mean by these vague words ('terrible', 'unbearable', 'crucial'). For example:

- What's 'terrible' about mistakes? If I did make one, what is the worst that could happen? What would the consequences be?

- What do I mean by 'unbearable'? If I imagine being rejected, what exactly comes to mind? What do I see happening? How do I think I would feel? And for how long?

- 'Crucial' in what way? What would happen if I were not on top of things? What does being on top protect me from? What is the worst that could happen if I was not? What sort of person would it make me? What impact would it have on my place in the world?

How will you know when you have found your rules?

Finding your personal rules is a fascinating process. You become like a detective searching for clues. You may even be quite surprised to discover what your rules are ('Oh, that's nonsense, I don't believe that'). If this is your first reaction, stop for a moment and consider. It may be hard to believe your rule when you are sitting calmly with it written down in front of you. But what about when you are in a situation relevant to it? For example, if your rule is to do with pleasing people, what about situations where you feel you have not done so? Or if your rule is to do with success, what about situations where you feel you have failed? Even if the rule you have identified does not seem fully convincing to you in the cold light of day, do you in fact *act and feel as if it were true?* If so, then – unlikely as it may seem – you've struck gold.

When it comes to identifying your rules, you already have a wealth of relevant information from the work you have done on anxious predictions, self-critical thoughts and enhancing self-acceptance. You may already have observed that certain situations always spark off uncomfortable emotions and cause you problems. These are likely to be the situations relevant to your own personal set of rules. The key situations for Jesse, for example, were times when he might be unable to perform to a high standard and feared he would attract criticism.

Your observation of repeating patterns in your reactions may have already given you a pretty clear idea of what your rules are. If not, don't worry. If you have never put your rules into words, then it may take a while to find the right phrasing. Be creative and open-minded. Approach the task from different angles, using the ideas below. Try different rules on for size, experiment with different wordings, and use all the clues at your disposal, until you find a general statement which seems to have been influencing you more or less consistently for some time, and which has affected your life in a range of different situations.

Although you may have a number of rules, it is probably best to work systematically on one at a time. Choose a rule that relates to an area of your life that you particularly want to change (e.g. relationships with other people). When you have completed the process of formulating an alternative rule and testing it out, you can use what you have learned to tackle other unhelpful rules that you also wish to change.

Sources of Information

You can use a number of sources of information to identify your rules:

1 Direct statements

2 Themes

3 Your judgements of yourself and other people

4 Memories, family sayings

5 Follow the opposite (things you feel really good about)

6 Downward arrow

---

1 Direct statements

- Look through the record you kept of your anxious predictions and self-critical thoughts in Part Two of the course, and see if you can identify any rules disguised as specific thoughts.

- Do any of your predictions in particular situations reflect broader issues?

- Are any of your self-critical thoughts specific examples of a more general rule?

_____

_____

_____

_____

_____

_____

2 Themes

- Even if no Rules for Living are directly stated in your record sheets, can you pick out continuing preoccupations and concerns? Or themes that run through the work you have done?

- What kinds of situations always make you doubt yourself (e.g. noticing you have not done something well, or having to encounter people you are unfamiliar with)?

- What aspects of yourself are you most hard on?

- What behaviour in other people undermines your confidence?

_____

_____

_____

_____

_____

_____

3 Your judgements of yourself and other people

- Look at your self-critical thoughts and ask yourself under what circumstances you begin to put yourself down?

- What do you criticize in yourself?

- What does that tell you about what you expect of yourself?

- What might happen if you relaxed your standards?

- How could things go wrong?

- If you do not keep a tight rein on yourself and obey the rule, where will you end up? What sort of person might you become (e.g. stupid, lazy, selfish)?

- What are you never allowed to do or be, no matter what?

- What standards do you expect other people to meet? (These may reflect the demands you place on yourself.)

_____

_____

_____

_____

_____

_____

_____

_____

_____

_____

_____

4 Memories, family sayings

Think back to when you were young, as a child and in your teens, and consider the messages you received about how to behave and the sort of person you should be. When you were growing up:

- What were you told you should and should not do?

- What were the consequences if you did not go along with what you were told? What sort of person did that make you? What were you told to expect? What were the implications for your relationships with other people, or for your future?

- What were you criticized or punished for?

- What did people say or do when you did not make the grade, or failed to meet expectations?

- How did people who were important to you react when you made mistakes, or were naughty, or did not do well at school?

- What were you praised and appreciated for?

- What did you have to do or be in order to receive warmth and affection?

- What family proverbs and sayings can you remember (e.g. 'Better safe than sorry', 'I want doesn't get', 'Stupid is as stupid does')?

To help you search out particular memories, look at your thought records again, and pick out feelings and thoughts that seem typical to you (themes). Ask yourself:

- When did you first have those feelings, or notice yourself thinking and behaving in that way? What were the circumstances?

- When you look at something that usually makes you anxious or triggers self-criticism, does this remind you of anything in your past? Whose voices or faces come to mind?

- When did you first grasp that certain things were expected of you, or get the sense that approval or love depended on something you were required to do or be, rather than simply on the fact that you existed?

- What particular memories or images or sayings come to mind?

_____

_____

_____

_____

_____

_____

_____

_____

_____

5 Follow the opposite

Think about the times when you have felt particularly good, and ask yourself:

- What makes you feel really, really good?

- What are the implications of this? What rule might you have obeyed? What standards did you meet?

- What qualities and actions do you really admire and value in other people? What does this tell you about how _you_ are supposed to act or be?

6 Downward arrow

This is a way of using your awareness of how you think and feel in specific problem situations to get at general rules. Here is Jesse's downward arrow, as an example:

Situation: Was asked a question I could not answer in a meeting.

Emotions: Anxious, self-conscious, embarrassed.

Thought: I should know the answer to that.

What does it mean to you that you don't?

↓

That I'm not doing my job properly.

↓

And if that was true, what would it mean to you?

↓

That sooner or later people will notice that I'm not up to it.

↓

And supposing they did, what would follow from that?

↓

I would lose credibility. I might be demoted.

↓

And what are the implications of all that for your performance?

↓

I really can't afford not to have the answers to everything.
I've got to come up with the goods, all the time, no matter what.

↓

So what's the rule?

↓

Unless I always get it right, I will never get anywhere in life.

You will find **Downward Arrow Charts** to fill in on pp. 17–19, and an extra one, at the back of the book which you can photocopy if you wish.

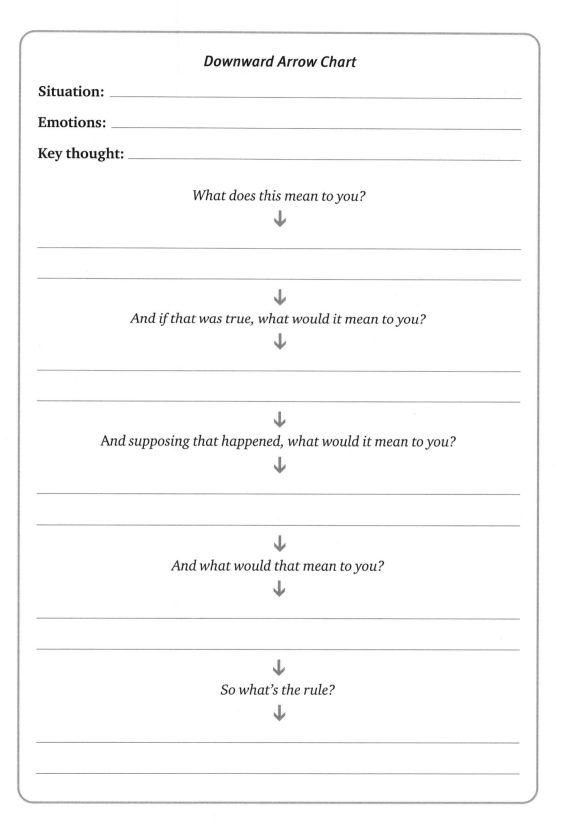

Downward Arrow Chart

Situation: _____

Emotions: _____

Key thought: _____

What does this mean to you?

↓

_____

_____

↓

And if that was true, what would it mean to you?

↓

_____

_____

↓

And supposing that happened, what would it mean to you?

↓

_____

_____

↓

And what would that mean to you?

↓

_____

_____

↓

So what's the rule?

↓

_____

_____

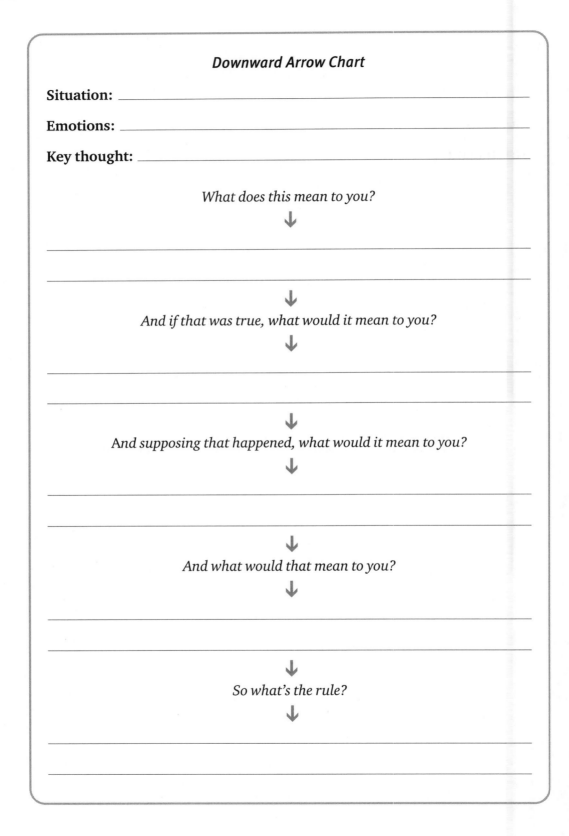

Downward Arrow Chart

Situation: _____

Emotions: _____

Key thought: _____

What does this mean to you?

↓

_____

_____

↓

And if that was true, what would it mean to you?

↓

_____

_____

↓

And supposing that happened, what would it mean to you?

↓

_____

_____

↓

And what would that mean to you?

↓

_____

_____

↓

So what's the rule?

↓

_____

_____

Downward Arrow Chart

Situation: _____

Emotions: _____

Key thought: _____

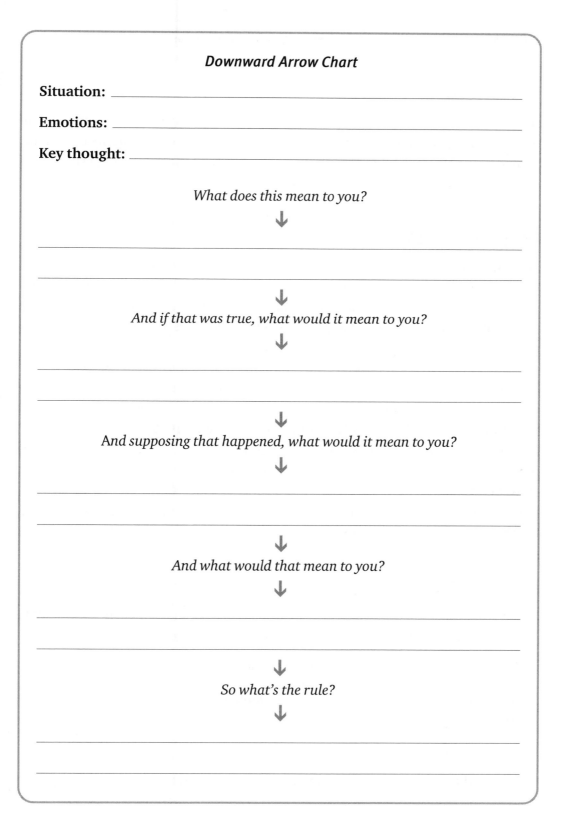

What does this mean to you?

↓

_____

_____

↓

And if that was true, what would it mean to you?

↓

_____

_____

↓

And supposing that happened, what would it mean to you?

↓

_____

_____

↓

And what would that mean to you?

↓

_____

_____

↓

So what's the rule?

↓

_____

_____

Some guidelines for using the Downward Arrow Charts:

How many steps?

Jesse reached his rule in five steps – but you may find it takes you more or less than that. Don't feel that you should have got there by a certain number of steps. Sometimes rules become clear to you very quickly, but other times not, especially if you have never really put your rules into words.

Starting point: Trigger situations

Start by thinking of the kind of problem situation that always upsets you and makes you feel bad about yourself (e.g. being criticized, failing to meet a deadline, avoiding an opportunity). These are the situations where your Bottom Line has been activated because you are in danger of breaking your rules, or have actually broken them.

Now think of a recent example that is still fresh in your memory. Write down the emotions you experienced in the situation and the thoughts or images that ran through your mind. Identify the thought or image which seems to you to be most important, and which most fully accounts for the emotions you experienced.

Then ask yourself: 'Supposing that thought or image were true, what would it mean to me?' When you find your answer to this question, ask the question again: 'And supposing that were true, what would it mean to me?' Continue on, step by step, until you discover the general underlying rule that makes sense of your thoughts and feelings in the specific problem situation you started from.

Helpful questions

'What would that mean to you?' is just one possible question you can use to pursue the downward arrow. Here are some others that may be helpful:

- Supposing that were true, what would it mean to you?

- Supposing that were true, what would happen then? What would follow from that?

- What are the implications of that?

- What's the worst that might happen? And what would happen then? And then?

- What would be so bad about that? (NB: 'I would feel bad' is not a helpful answer to this question. You probably would feel bad, but that does not tell you anything useful or interesting about your rules. So if your immediate answer is something about your own feelings, ask yourself *why* you would feel bad.)

- How would that be a problem for you?

- What does that tell you about how you should behave?

- What does that tell you about what you expect from yourself, or from other people?

- What does that tell you about your standards for yourself?

- What does that tell you about the sort of person you should be in order to feel good about yourself?

- What does that tell you about what you must do or be, in order to gain the acceptance, approval, liking or love of other people?

- What does that tell you about what you must do or be in order to succeed in life?

Recognizing when you have reached the rule

If, when you do the downward arrow, you have a sense of going round in circles after a certain point, the chances are that you have reached your rule, but that it is not in a form you can easily recognize. In this case, stop questioning, stand back and reflect on your sequence. What Rule for Living do the final levels suggest to you? When you have an idea, try the draft rule on for size. Can you think of other situations where this might apply? Does it make sense of how you operate elsewhere?

Try another similar starting point. Does it end up in the same place? Take a few days to observe yourself, especially your anxious predictions and self-critical thoughts. Does your draft rule make sense of your everyday reactions? If so, you are in a position to start looking for a more helpful alternative. If not, what rule might better account for what you observe? Don't be discouraged; have another go.

You may find at first that you have a good general sense of what your rule might be, but that the way you have expressed it doesn't feel quite right. If so, play around with the wording until you find a version that 'clicks' with you. Try out the different possible forms a rule can take: assumptions, drivers and value judgements. When you get the right wording, you will experience a sense of recognition – 'Aha! So that's what it is.'

Remember, you may well have a number of unhelpful Rules for Living – people often do. In this case, you might find it interesting to pursue downward arrow from several different starting points. This is crucial if you have difficulty identifying your rule when you first do it. It is also a way of checking that you are on the right track, and of discovering your other rules. Experiment with asking different questions, too. The answers may be illuminating.

How do Rules for Living affect your everyday life?

Rules may influence how you think, feel and act in a whole range of different situations, and over time. As we said, you may well have learned them when you were very young.

Once you have identified an unhelpful rule, it is worth considering the impact it has had on your life. When you come to change your rule, you will not only need to formulate an alternative, more realistic and helpful Rule for Living, but also to modify its continued influence on your daily life. Recognizing the old rule's impact will help you to achieve this. You will already have much of the information you need, from the work you have done on anxious predictions, self-critical thoughts and enhancing self-esteem.

Start by looking at your life now. Ask yourself:

How does your rule affect your relationships?

_____

_____

_____

_____

_____

_____

_____

_____

_____

Does it affect your study or your work?

_____

_____

_____

_____

_____

_____

How does it affect how you spend your leisure time?

_____

_____

_____

_____

_____

How does it affect how well you look after yourself?

_____

_____

_____

_____

_____

_____

_____

How does it affect how you react when things don't go well?

_____

_____

_____

_____

_____

_____

How does it affect how you respond to opportunities and challenges?

_____

_____

_____

_____

_____

_____

How does it affect how good you are at expressing your feelings and making sure your needs are met?

_____

_____

_____

_____

_____

_____

_____

How do you know your rule is in operation? What are the clues?

_____

_____

_____

_____

_____

_____

What emotions do you experience?

_____

_____

_____

_____

_____

_____

_____

What sensations do you notice in your body?

_____

_____

_____

_____

_____

_____

_____

What usually runs through your mind (thoughts, images)?

_____

_____

_____

_____

_____

_____

What do you do (or fail to do)?

_____

_____

_____

_____

_____

_____

What reactions do you get from other people?

_____

_____

_____

_____

_____

_____

Now look back over time. Can you see a similar pattern extending into your past? What effect has the rule had on you, over the course of your life?

What unnecessary precautions has it led you to take?

_____

_____

_____

_____

_____

_____

What have you missed out on, or failed to take advantage of, or lost because of the rule?

_____

_____

_____

_____

_____

_____

What restrictions has it placed on you?

_____

_____

_____

_____

_____

How has it stopped you appreciating yourself and relaxing with others?

_____

_____

_____

_____

_____

How has it affected your ability to experience pleasure?

_____

_____

_____

_____

_____

Look back at the work you have already done on anxious predictions, self-critical thinking and self-acceptance. How much of what you have observed can be accounted for by this rule?

_____

_____

_____

_____

_____

_____

_____

After this detailed investigation, you should now have a good sense of what your rule (or rules) might be. Use the first three headings on the worksheet on p. 40 to summarize in writing what you have discovered:

1 My old rule is (state the rule in your own words):

2 This rule has had the following impact on my life (summarize the ways in which it has affected you):

3 I know the rule is in operation, because (note the clues that tell you your rule is active – feelings, thoughts, patterns of behaviour):

How can you find new Rules for Living?

Now that you know what your rules are, you need to start changing them. Here are some questions that may be helpful:

- Where did the rule come from?

- In what ways is the rule unreasonable?

- What are the advantages of obeying the rule?

- What are the disadvantages of obeying the rule?

- How can you chart the advantages and disadvantages?

- What alternative rule would be more realistic and helpful?

Your aim is to find new rules that will encourage you to adopt more realistic standards for yourself and help you to get what you want out of life. As we said earlier, you may have discovered more than one unhelpful rule that keeps your self-esteem low (for example, perhaps you need approval and you are also something of a perfectionist). If so, start with the one you would most like to change, and then use what you learn to undermine the others. You will gain more from working systematically on one rule at a time rather than jumping around from one to another.

Use the spaces provided to note down your ideas in detail. Then, just as you did with your investigations earlier on, summarize your thoughts on the worksheet on pp. 40–2.

1 Where did the rule come from?

The purpose here is not to wallow in the past, but to understand how your rules started and what has kept them going. This will help you detach yourself from them. Keep these questions in mind:

- How far does my past experience explain my rules?

- How well does it explain the strategies I have adopted?

- How well does it help me to understand how I operate now?

Understanding the origins of your rules will help you to see that they were your best options, given the knowledge available to you at the time. This insight can be a helpful first step towards updating your Rules for Living. However, if you cannot think where your rules have come from, do not despair. This information is not essential to changing them. It just means that the questions that follow are likely to be more helpful to you.

If you can, summarize for yourself the experiences in your life that led to the rule. Remind yourself when you first noticed the signs that tell you it is in operation.

- Was the rule part of your family culture, or part of the wider culture in which you grew up?

- Did you adopt it as a means of dealing with difficult and distressing circumstances?

- Was it a way of gaining the closeness and caring you needed as a child?

- Or was it a way of managing unkind or unpredictable adults?

- Or coping with the demands of school?

- Or avoiding teasing and ridicule?

_____

_____

_____

_____

_____

_____

You may also want to take into account later experiences that have helped to keep the rule in place.

- For example, have you found yourself trapped in abusive relationships?

- Have other people taken over the critical role your parents took towards you?

- Have you repeatedly found yourself in situations that reinforce the policies you have adopted?

_____

_____

_____

_____

_____

_____

_____

Even though the rule did make sense at one point, you nevertheless need to ask yourself how relevant it is to you now, as an adult.

- Is it still necessary or beneficial?

- Or might you in fact be better off with an updated perspective?

_____

_____

_____

_____

_____

_____

2 In what ways is the rule unreasonable?

Call on your adult knowledge to consider in what ways your rule fails to take account of how the world works.

- How does it go beyond what is realistically possible for an ordinary, imperfect human being?

- How does it go beyond what you would expect from another person you respected and cared about?

- In what ways are its demands over the top, exaggerated or impossible to meet?

_____

_____

_____

_____

_____

_____

Remember, this was a contract you made with yourself as a child.

- Would you now allow a child to run your life for you?

- Why not?

- What can you see as an adult that you could not grasp when you were very young?

_____

_____

_____

_____

_____

_____

3 What are the advantages of obeying the rule?

It is important to be clear about the benefits of following your present rules, because the alternatives you formulate will need to give you the advantages of the old rule, without its disadvantages. Otherwise, you may be understandably reluctant to change.

Make a list of the advantages of your present rule.

- What benefits do you gain from it?
- In what ways is it helpful to you?
- What might you risk if you were to let go of it?
- What does it protect you from?

_____

_____

_____

_____

_____

_____

_____

People often worry that if they were to abandon their rules, catastrophe would follow. For instance, Jesse suspected that if he were not a perfectionist, he might never again do a decent piece of work. It felt to him as though his perfectionism was the only thing that guaranteed acceptance from other people. Ideas like these can be tested out through experiments at a later stage. For the moment, the important thing is to identify the advantages and fears that keep the old rule in place.

When you have listed all the advantages of your rule, take a careful look at them. Some of them may be more apparent than real. For example, the rule that you must always put others first may encourage you to be genuinely helpful, and dispose others to feel kindly towards you. But there may be a downside: your own needs are not met, and you may end up feeling increasingly resentful and exhausted, so that in the end you are no longer in a fit state to look after others. For instance, Jesse realized, on reflection, that his excellent work did not in fact always guarantee acceptance. He was sometimes so driven and tense that people found him unapproachable and thought him arrogant.

Do not take the advantages you have identified for granted. Look at them closely, and assess how genuine they are. Do the same for your concerns about dropping your rule.

- How do you know these things would actually happen?

- How could you find out?

_____

_____

_____

_____

_____

_____

_____

_____

4 What are the disadvantages of obeying the rule?

You have explored the apparent advantages; now for the disadvantages. Examine the ways in which the rule robs you of pleasure, sours your relationships with other people, undermines your sense of achievement or stands in the way of getting what you want out of life. Use the information you collected when you were assessing its impact on your life (see pp. 27–8).

_____

_____

_____

_____

_____

_____

_____

Make a list of some of your main goals in life (e.g. to have a satisfying career; to take pleasure in what you do; to be relaxed and confident with people; to make the most of every experience). Then ask yourself:

- Does this rule help me to achieve these goals?

- Is it the best strategy for getting what I want out of life?

- Or does it in fact stand in my way?

_____

_____

_____

_____

_____

_____

_____

_____

_____

5 How can you chart the advantages and disadvantages?

Use the chart on the next page. Summarize the advantages and disadvantages you have identified by writing the apparent advantages attached to your rule and the apparent risks of letting it go, in the left-hand column. Then list its disadvantages, in the right-hand column.

Now weigh up the two lists and write your conclusions about just how helpful your rule is underneath. If you decide that, on balance, your rule is helpful, then you need take this exercise no further. If, on the other hand, you conclude that the rule is _un_helpful, and stands in the way of getting what you want out of life, you need to formulate an alternative that will give you the advantages of the old rule without its disadvantages.

Advantages of the rule

Disadvantages of the rule

Conclusions

6 What alternative rule would be more realistic and helpful?

New rules can transform day-to-day experiences. They allow you to deal comfortably and confidently with situations that, under the old system, would have triggered anxiety or self-criticism. What would have been disasters become passing inconveniences. What would have seemed matters of life and death become exciting challenges and opportunities.

It's worth remembering...

New rules open the door to accepting yourself and achieving what you want out of life.

To help you to free up your thinking, consider whether you would advise another person to adopt your old rule as a policy. Would you want to pass on your rule to a good friend, or to your children, if you had any? If not, what would you prefer their rule to be?

Your new rule will probably be more flexible and realistic than the old one. It will inhabit the middle ground rather than the extremes. So it may begin:

- 'I want…'
- 'I enjoy…'
- 'I prefer…'
- 'It's OK to…'

rather than:

- 'I must…'
- 'I should…'
- 'I ought to…'
- 'It would be terrible if…'

You may find that your new rule starts with the same 'If…', but ends with a different 'then…' For example, Jesse replaced 'If someone criticizes me, it means I have failed' with 'If someone criticizes me, I may or may not deserve it. If I have done something worthy of criticism, that's not failure – it's all part of being human, and there's nothing wrong with that.'

This example illustrates something typical of new rules: they are often longer and more elaborate than old ones. This is because they are based on an adult's ability to understand how the world works, and to take into account variations in circumstances. Sometimes it is nice, however, to capture their essence in a slogan, the sort of snappy statement you might find on a badge or T-shirt. Some time after he had formulated his new rule, Jesse watched a film in which a young boy was struggling to please his father on the mistaken grounds that only something exceptional would win his approval. Jesse decided to adopt the father's loving response as a slogan for himself: 'You don't have to be great, to be great.'

You may find it difficult at first to find an alternative you feel comfortable with. Write down your best shot, and then try putting it into operation for a week or two to find out how well it works for you and if there are any ways of changing it for the better. It may also be worth talking to and observing other people. What do you think their rules might be? Your observations will give you an opportunity to discover the different positions people adopt, and to clarify what strategy might work best for you.

How can you put your new Rules for Living into practice?

Your old rule may have been in operation for a long time. In contrast, the new one is freshly made, and it may take a while for it to become a comfortable fit. Now you need to consolidate your new policy, check out how well it works for you, and start putting it into practice in your everyday life. This takes us back to all the work you have already done, and to the central idea of finding things out for yourself by setting up experiments and examining their outcomes. The most important thing you can do to strengthen your new rule (and indeed to discover if you need to make further changes to it) is to act as if it was true and observe the outcome. Here are some ideas on how to go about this.

The written summary

This is a good time to complete your written summary, using the headings on the worksheet on pp. 40–2. The summary will give you a concise version of the work you have done, which you can then easily review and refer to as you continue to work on finding more flexible rules.

You have already summarized your findings in relation to recognizing the rule and its impact on your life. Now continue with the work you have done on investigating where it came from, its shortcomings, and your new rule:

1 It is understandable that I have this rule because (summarize the experiences that led to the development of the rule and that have reinforced it):

2 However the rule is unreasonable because (summarize the ways in which your rule does not fit the way the world works):

3 The advantages of obeying the rule are (summarize the advantages of obeying the rule and the risks of letting it go. Check to see if these are genuine):

4 But the disadvantages are (summarize the harmful effects of obeying the rule):

5 A more realistic and helpful rule would be (write out your new rule, in your own words):

6 In order to test-drive the new rule, I need to (write down how you plan to strengthen your new rule and act on it in everyday life).

Like your list of positive qualities and good points, a written summary on its own is not enough. Your new rule needs to be part of your everyday awareness, so that it has the best possible chance of influencing your feelings and thoughts and what you do in problem situations. So when you have completed your summary, put it somewhere easily accessible and, over the next few weeks, read it carefully every day – perhaps more than once a day, to begin with. A good time is just after you get up. This puts you in the right frame of mind for the day. Another good time is just before you go to bed, when you can think over your day and consider how the work you have done is changing things for you.

The objective is to make your new rule part of your mental furniture so that acting in accordance with it eventually becomes second nature. Continue to read your summary regularly until you find you have reached this point.

The flashcard

Another helpful way to encourage the changes you are trying to make is to write your new rule on a stiff card (an index card, for example) that is small enough to be easily carried in a wallet or purse. You can use the card to remind you of the new strategies you aim to adopt, by taking it out and reading it carefully when you have a quiet moment in the day, and before you enter situations you know are likely to be problematic for you.

Changing the Rules: My Summary

1 My old rule is:

2 This rule has had the following impact on my life:

3 I know that the rule is in operation because:

4 It is understandable that I have this rule, because:

5 However, the rule is unreasonable, because:

6 The advantages of obeying the rule are:

7 But the disadvantages are:

8 A more realistic and helpful rule would be:

9 In order to test-drive the new rule, I need to:

Dealing with the old rule

Even when you have a well-formulated alternative and you are beginning to act on it, your old rule may still rear its ugly head in the usual situations for a while. After all, it has been around for a long time and may not just slink quietly away as soon as you expose it to the light of day. If you are prepared for this, you will be able to tackle the old rule calmly when you see it in operation. This is where the work you did in Part Two, on anxious predictions and self-critical thoughts, will pay off. Remember that these are signs that your old rule is in danger of being broken. Keep using the skills you learned to question your thoughts, find alternatives to them, and experiment with acting in different ways. Over time, you will find that you have less and less need to do so.

Experimenting with your new rule

Start acting in accordance with your new rule and observing the outcome. Do the 'If …' or 'Unless…' and see if the 'then…' follows. If you look back over this workbook and Part Two, you may well find that you have already been putting your new rule into practice when you checked out anxious thoughts, combated self-criticism by being kinder and more tolerant towards yourself, focused on your good points, gave yourself credit for your achievements, and treated yourself with care and respect. Examine what you have already done, and identify times when your new rule has been in operation.

In addition, you need to ensure that your new rule is indeed a useful policy, and explore its impact on your everyday life. This means expanding your boundaries, discovering that it is still possible to feel good about yourself even if you are less than perfect, even if some people dislike and disapprove of you, even if you sometimes put yourself first, or even if you are sometimes gloriously out of control.

Make sure that you include specific changes in how you go about things, not just general strategies. Not just 'be more assertive', for example, but 'ask for help when I need it', 'say no when I disagree with someone', 'refuse requests when to carry them out would be very costly for me', 'be open about my thoughts and feelings with people I know well'. Then consider how to include these changes in your life. You could, for instance, use your **Daily Activity Diary** (see Part Two) to plan experiments at specific times, with specific people, in specific situations. Or you could use the **Experimenting with New Rules Worksheet** on pp. 44–50. There is also a worksheet at the back of the book, which you can photocopy if you wish.

Experimenting with New Rules Worksheet

Date/time	The situation	What I did	The outcome (what I noticed, felt, thought, learned)

Experimenting with New Rules Worksheet

Date/time	The situation	What I did	The outcome (what I noticed, felt, thought, learned)

Experimenting with New Rules Worksheet

Date/time	The situation	What I did	The outcome (what I noticed, felt, thought, learned)

Experimenting with New Rules Worksheet

Date/time	The situation	What I did	The outcome (what I noticed, felt, thought, learned)

Experimenting with New Rules Worksheet

Date/time	The situation	What I did	The outcome (what I noticed, felt, thought, learned)

Experimenting with New Rules Worksheet

Date/time	The situation	What I did	The outcome (what I noticed, felt, thought, learned)

Experimenting with New Rules Worksheet

Date/time	The situation	What I did	The outcome (what I noticed, felt, thought, learned)

Make sure you assess the results of your experiments, just as you did when you were checking out anxious predictions. After each experiment, ask yourself:

- What are the signs that your new rule is working?

- What are the signs that your new rule is *not* working?

- What have you observed in yourself (e.g. your feelings, your body state, changes in your behaviour) that tells you the new rule is working (or not)?

- What have you seen in other people's reactions to you when you are following the new rule?

Don't be surprised if acting in accordance with your new rule feels uncomfortable at first. You may well feel quite apprehensive before you carry out experiments. If so, work out what you are predicting and use your experiment to check it out. (Remember to drop unnecessary precautions, otherwise you will not get the information you need.) Equally, you may find you feel guilty or worried after you have carried out an experiment, even if it has gone well. This happens, for example, with people who are experimenting with being less self-sacrificing or with dropping their standards from '110 per cent' to 'good enough'. Or again, you may get angry with yourself and become self-critical if you plan to carry out an experiment and then chicken out. If you experience uncomfortable feelings like these, look for the thoughts behind them and answer them, using the skills you have already learned.

Be prepared

It could take as much as six to eight months for your new rule to take over completely. As long as the new rule is useful to you and you can see it taking you in useful and interesting directions, don't give up. You may find it helpful to review your progress regularly and to set yourself targets. Ask yourself, for example:

- What have I achieved in the last week?

- What have I achieved in the last month?

- What do I want to aim for in the next week?

- What do I want to aim for in the next month?

Keeping written records of your experiments and their outcomes, and of unhelpful thoughts that you have tackled along the way, will help you to see how things are progressing. You can also look back over what you have done and use it as a source of encouragement.

Summary

1 When you have low self-esteem, unhelpful Rules for Living prevent you from getting what you want out of life and accepting yourself as you are.

2 Rules are learned through experience and observation. They are part of the culture we grow up in, and they are usually passed on to us by our families.

3 Many rules are helpful. But the unhelpful rules linked to low self-esteem are rigid, demanding and extreme, they restrict freedom of movement, and make change and growth difficult or impossible.

4 Rules are a way of coping with the apparent truth of your Bottom Line, but they do nothing to change it. In fact, they help to keep it in place.

5 You can identify and change unhelpful rules. Then you can formulate new, more realistic and helpful rules, and experiment with acting on them to make sure that they work for you.

SECTION 2: Creating a New Bottom Line

You have now laid the foundations for tackling your Bottom Line (the negative beliefs about yourself that lie at the heart of low self-esteem). It could be that, after the work that you have done on your anxious and self-critical thoughts, on self-acceptance and on formulating new Rules for Living, your ideas about yourself have already changed – your Old Bottom Line may already look less convincing than it did. In this section, capitalizing on what you have already done, you will learn how to undermine your Old Bottom Line and how to create a new, more accepting and kindly alternative.

This section will help you understand:

- how to identify your Old Bottom Line
- how to create a more positive and accepting New Bottom Line
- how to question the 'evidence' that appears to support your Old Bottom Line
- how to gather evidence to support your New Bottom Line
- how to use observation and experiments to strengthen your New Bottom Line

How can you identify your old Bottom Line?

Having made your way through the first two workbooks, you have probably already gained a pretty good idea of what your Bottom Line is. These are some possible sources of information that will help you identify it more clearly:

1 Your knowledge of your own history

2 The fears expressed in your anxious predictions

3 Your self-critical thoughts

4 Thoughts that make it hard for you to focus on your good points

5 The imagined consequences of breaking your old rules

6 The Downward Arrow (see this workbook Section 1, p. 17)

Even if you are already pretty sure of what your Bottom Line is, reviewing each source of information in turn will enable you to fine-tune the wording and perhaps discover other negative beliefs about yourself that you were less aware of. It is quite possible that you have more than one Bottom Line. If so, choose the Bottom Line that seems most important, and work on that. You can then use what you have learned to change other negative beliefs if you wish. Write down whatever hunches about your Bottom Line come to mind as you consider each potential source of information.

1 Your knowledge of your own history

When you read the people's case studies in Part One, did any of them echo experiences you had when you were growing up? Even if they didn't, did you find yourself thinking back to when you were young and remembering things that happened to you?

You can use these memories to clarify your Bottom Line. In particular, consider:

- What early experiences encouraged you to think badly of yourself? What events in your childhood and adolescence led you to conclude that you were somehow lacking as a person?

- When did you first have this feeling about yourself? Do you remember specific events or incidents? Or was there a general atmosphere of unkindness, or disapproval and criticism, or lack of affection?

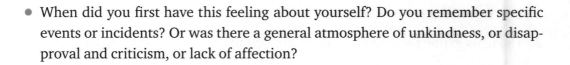

● Whose voice do you hear when you are being hard on yourself? Whose face comes to mind? What messages did this person (or these people) give you about the kind of person you are?

_____

_____

_____

_____

_____

● What words were used to describe you when you failed to please or attracted criticism? (The words used by others may have become your own words for yourself.)

_____

_____

_____

_____

_____

2 The fears expressed in your anxious predictions

Think back to the work you did on your anxious predictions. Your fears, and the unnecessary precautions you took to keep yourself safe, could give you clues about your Bottom Line.

● Supposing what you most feared had come true. What sort of person would that have made you?

_____

_____

_____

_____

_____

- And what about your unnecessary precautions? What sort of person did you fear might be revealed if you did not take steps to conceal yourself?

_____

_____

_____

_____

_____

_____

3 Your self-critical thoughts

Look back over the work you did on combating your self-critical thoughts. These thoughts may be a direct reflection of your Bottom Line.

- What words did you use to describe yourself when you were being self-critical? What names did you call yourself? Look for repeating patterns. What negative beliefs about yourself do your self-critical thoughts reflect?

_____

_____

_____

_____

_____

- How similar are these words to words that were used about you by other people when you were small?

_____

_____

_____

_____

_____

● When you do things that trigger self-criticism, what do those things suggest about you as a person? What sort of person would do things like that?

_____

_____

_____

_____

_____

4 Thoughts that make it hard for you to accept your good points

Examine the doubts and reservations that came to mind when you were trying to list your good points and observe them in action in Part Two, Section 3.

● What thoughts made you reluctant to accept positive aspects of yourself?

_____

_____

_____

_____

_____

_____

● How did you disqualify or discount your good points?

_____

_____

_____

_____

_____

_____

● What objections did you raise to giving yourself credit for your achievements, and treating yourself to relaxation and pleasure?

_____

_____

_____

_____

_____

_____

● What beliefs about yourself do these doubts, reservations and disclaimers reflect?

_____

_____

_____

_____

_____

_____

5 The imagined consequences of breaking your old rules

Go back to the Rules for Living that you identified in Section 1 of this workbook (pp. 8–29), and look at what you imagined would happen if you broke them.

● If you break your Rules for Living, what does that say about you as a person?

_____

_____

_____

_____

_____

- What kind of person makes mistakes, fails to win everyone's approval, loses their grip on their emotions, or whatever your rules demand of you?

6 The Downward Arrow

Let's take Briony, from Part One, as an example of how to use the downward arrow technique to identify the Bottom Line. Here is Briony's case study:

CASE STUDY: Briony

Briony was adopted by her father's brother and his wife after both her parents were killed in a car crash when she was seven. Her new step-parents already had two older daughters. Briony became the family scapegoat. Everything that went wrong was blamed on her. Briony was a loving little girl, who liked to please people. She tried desperately to be good, but nothing worked. Every day she faced new punishments. She was deprived of contact with friends, made to give up music – which she loved – and was forced to do more than her fair share of work around the house. Briony became more and more confused. She could not understand why everything she did was wrong.

One night, when she was eleven, Briony's stepfather came silently into her room in the middle of the night. He put his hand over her mouth and raped her. He told her that she was dirty and disgusting, that she had asked for it, and that if she told anyone what had happened, no one would believe her, because they all knew she was a filthy little liar. Afterwards, she crept around the house in terror. No one seemed to notice or care. Briony's doubts about herself crystallized into a firm belief at that point. She was bad. Other people could see it, and would treat her accordingly.

And here is Briony's Downward Arrow, leading to her Bottom Line:

Situation: New friend promised to phone and did not do so

Emotions: Sick to my stomach, despairing

Key Thought: He's forgotten

If that was true, what would it mean about you?

↓

That I'm not worth remembering

↓

And what would that tell you about yourself?

↓

That he's backed off because he's seen the real me

↓

If he had, what would he have seen?

↓

Something he didn't like

↓

What would that be? What would he not like?

↓

The real me, that doesn't deserve to be liked

↓

If that was true, what would it say about you as a person?

↓

I'm bad

You can now use the 'Downward Arrow' technique to identify your own Bottom Line, using the worksheet on p. 61.

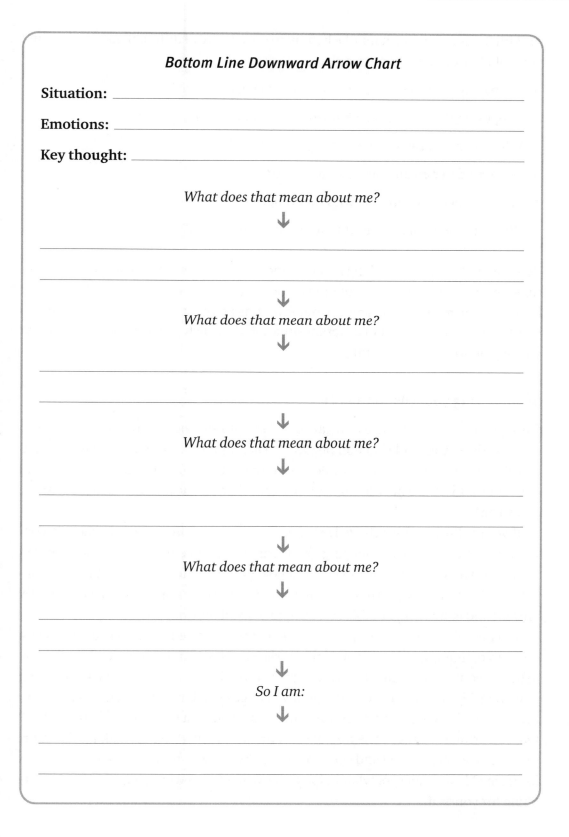

Bottom Line Downward Arrow Chart

Situation: _____

Emotions: _____

Key thought: _____

What does that mean about me?

↓

_____

_____

↓

What does that mean about me?

↓

_____

_____

↓

What does that mean about me?

↓

_____

_____

↓

What does that mean about me?

↓

_____

_____

↓

So I am:

↓

_____

_____

As with Rules for Living, it may be helpful to use a range of different questions to find your Old Bottom Line, for example:

- Supposing that was true, what would it mean about me?
- Supposing that was true, what would it tell me about myself?
- What does that say about me as a person?
- What kind of person does that make me?
- What beliefs about myself does that reflect?
- What are the implications of that for how I see myself?

Remember that you are looking for an opinion about yourself that you have held over time and in many different situations. You may wish to confirm your findings (or have another go, if you are having trouble finding your Bottom Line, or putting it into words) by using a number of different situations in which you usually feel bad about yourself as your starting point.

Summarizing your Old Bottom Line

Once you have a clear sense of what your Old Bottom Line is, write it down in your own words on the worksheet on pp. 93–4. Then rate how far you believe it, from 0 to 100 per cent (100 per cent would mean that you still find it fully convincing; 50 per cent that you are in two minds; 5 per cent that you now hardly believe it at all, and so on).

If your self-esteem is relatively strong, your Bottom Line may only become convincing in particularly challenging situations. If so, make two ratings: how far you believe it when it is at its strongest, and how far you believe it when it is least convincing. Alternatively, you may find that your Bottom Line is more or less consistently present and convincing. In this case, you may need only one rating.

You may also find that your degree of belief has changed since you began to work on overcoming low self-esteem. If this is the case for you, write down how far you believed your Bottom Line before you started the book, and how far you believe it now. Consider too what accounts for any changes you have observed. Was it learning to face things that frightened you and discovering that the worst did not happen? Was it learning to escape the trap of self-critical thinking? Was it making the effort to focus on what is strong and good in yourself? Or was it finding more flexible Rules for Living? If you can spot what helped, this will tell you what you need to continue doing for yourself.

How can you create a new, more positive and accepting Bottom Line?

Over time, you have probably accumulated a sizeable 'bank account' of negatively biased thoughts and memories that seem to support your Old Bottom Line. You can call on your 'Old Bottom Line Account' any time you want to, add new deposits, withdraw items and dwell on them like a miser counting and recounting money.

In contrast, creating a New Bottom Line opens an account in favour of yourself. It gives you a place to store experiences that contradict your Old Bottom Line and support a new, more kindly perspective. You have somewhere you can keep positive aspects of yourself safe, knowing that you can call on them when you need them.

The work you did in earlier workbooks may have given you some idea of what your New Bottom Line might be. As you checked out anxious predictions, combated self-critical thoughts, focused on positive aspects of yourself and changed your personal rules, what new ideas about yourself came to mind?

- When you look back over all you have done in each of these areas, what do the changes you have made tell you about yourself? Are they entirely consistent with your old negative view?

_____

_____

_____

_____

_____

_____

- Do the qualities, strengths, assets and skills you have observed fit with your Old Bottom Line?

_____

_____

_____

_____

_____

- Or do they suggest that it is a biased, unfair point of view that fails to take account of what is good and strong and worthy in you?

_____

_____

_____

_____

- What perspective on yourself would better account for _everything_ you have observed?

_____

_____

_____

_____

_____

- What New Bottom Line would acknowledge that, like the rest of the human race, you are short of perfect, but that – along with your weaknesses and flaws – you have strengths and qualities?

_____

_____

_____

_____

_____

Your New Bottom Line may be the opposite of your Old Bottom Line (e.g. 'I am bad' ➡ 'I am good', or 'I am unworthy' ➡ 'I am worthy'). Or it may, so to speak, 'jump the tracks' and go off in a new direction which pretty much makes the Old Bottom Line irrelevant (e.g. 'I am worthless' ➡ 'I belong', or 'I am rubbish' ➡ 'I am a human being'). The key thing is to find a New Bottom Line that makes sense to you personally, and holds the promise of changing how you feel about yourself.

> ### It's worth remembering...
>
> You are the judge and jury, not the counsel for the prosecution.
> Your job is to take *all* the evidence into account, not just the evidence in
> favour of condemning the prisoner.

You may find that a New Bottom Line immediately springs to mind when you think back over everything you have done. Or your mind may be pretty much a blank, especially if your low self-esteem has been in place for a long time and you have a strong taboo on thinking well of yourself which still needs to be challenged.

Do not worry if this is the case. Your ideas will probably become clearer as you continue through the workbook. For the moment, it may be helpful to ask yourself: 'If I were not ____ [your Old Bottom Line], what would I like to be?' For example, 'If I were not incompetent, I would like to be competent.'

Try this for yourself:

'If I were not _____

I would like to be _____ '

Countering all-or-nothing thinking

Remember that this workbook is not about the power of positive thinking, or about encouraging you to become as unrealistically positive about yourself as you were unrealistically negative. It is about achieving a balanced, unbiased view of yourself, which puts your weaknesses and flaws in the context of a broadly favourable perspective, and aims for 'good enough' rather than 'perfect'.

Let us consider this in relation to the New Bottom Line 'I am likeable':

1 Imagine a line representing likeability:

_____

0%   100%

Someone at the extreme right-hand end of the line would be 100 per cent likeable, while someone at the extreme left-hand end would be 0 per cent likeable.

2 Right now, put a cross on the line where you think you fall. If you have doubts about how likeable you are, you probably fall towards the left-hand end of the line.

Now consider what '0 per cent likeable' and '100 per cent likeable' actually mean.

In order to be '0 per cent likeable', you would have to be:	**In order to be '100 per cent likeable', you would have to be:**
• *Never* likeable, ever	• Likeable *all the time*
• *Completely* unlikeable (nothing about you could be at all likeable)	• *Completely* likeable (nothing about you could be at all unlikeable)
• Not likeable to *anyone*	• Likeable to *everyone*

Looking at it this way, you can probably see that to be 0 per cent or 100 per cent likeable is pretty much impossible. Nobody could be that dreadful – or that perfect.

3 Think now about someone you know. With the extremes (0 and 100 per cent) clearly in mind, where would you put him or her on the line?

0%   100%

4 And, once again, keeping the extremes in mind, where would you now put yourself?

0%   100%

When you decide on your New Bottom Line, keep this point in mind. You are not looking for the unattainable 100 per cent, you are looking for 'good enough'.

Summarizing your New Bottom Line

When you have a sense of what it is, write down your New Bottom Line on the worksheet on pp. 93–4. Rate how far you believe it, just as you rated your belief in your Old Bottom Line, including variations in how convincing it seems to you and how your belief has changed since you began to work on overcoming your low self-esteem. Then take a moment to focus your attention on it, and note what emotions come up and how strong they are. As you continue through the workbook, come back to this summary from time to time, and observe how your belief in your New Bottom Line changes as you focus on evidence that supports and strengthens it.

Don't worry if, for the moment, your belief in your New Bottom Line is low. If your Old Bottom Line has been in place for a long time, it will take patience and practice to make the new one powerfully convincing. We'll now move on to consider how to undermine your Old Bottom Line further, and how to strengthen the New Bottom Line you have started to identify.

What evidence appears to support your Old Bottom Line?

Your negative beliefs about yourself are based on experience – an attempt to make sense of what has happened to you. This means that, as you look back over your life, you are likely to see lots of 'evidence' that seems to support them. (Remember that, thanks to biased thinking, you are likely to have noticed and remembered what seemed to support your negative beliefs, and to have screened out or discounted what did not fit.) Examining this so-called 'evidence' – and searching for other ways to explain it – is the next step towards overcoming low self-esteem.

What sources of 'evidence' might seem to support your Old Bottom Line?

Reflect for a moment on your Old Bottom Line and ask yourself:

- What experiences, past and present, come to mind?

- What events appear to support it?

- What makes you say that you are inadequate, unlikeable, incompetent, or whatever your Bottom Line may be?

- What leads you to reach such negative conclusions about yourself?

Supporting 'evidence' varies from person to person. Sometimes most of it is found in the past, in relationships or experiences. However, more recent events can also be used as sources of evidence. Some common sources are listed, with examples, below. Which of these ring bells for you?

Common Sources of 'Evidence'

1 Current difficulties and symptoms of distress

2 Failure to overcome current difficulties alone

3 Past errors and failures

4 Specific shortcomings

5 Physical characteristics

6 Psychological characteristics   *continues on next page*

7 Differences between yourself and other people

8 Other people's behaviour towards you, past or present

9 The behaviour of others for whom you feel responsible

10 Loss of something that was a part of your identity

Use this section as an opportunity to reflect on the sources of 'evidence' you are using to support your Old Bottom Line. Tick the ones you recognize.

1 Current difficulties and symptoms of distress

People with low self-esteem may have a range of difficulties and symptoms. For example, low self-esteem might sometimes make you feel quite depressed. You may then find it hard to gear yourself up to do anything. This could make you see yourself as lazy. In other words, you might see your depression as yet another sign of what a bad person you are, rather than a temporary symptom of an understandable state, which will disappear once your mood lifts.

Does this sound familiar? ☐

2 Failure to overcome current difficulties alone

You might see being unable to manage independently as a sign of weakness or failure, rather than a sensible recognition that two heads are sometimes better than one and that everyone needs help at times. This could have prevented you from asking for the support you needed from partners, relatives or friends.

Does this sound familiar? ☐

3 Past errors and failures

From time to time, we are all selfish, thoughtless, irritable, or less than fully honest. We all take short cuts, make mistakes, avoid challenges and fail to achieve objectives. Perhaps you would see such actions as evidence of basic inadequacy rather than normal human weakness?

Does this sound familiar? ☐

4 Specific shortcomings

No one is perfect. We all have aspects of ourselves that we would like to change or improve. Would you see these shortcomings as further proof that there is something fundamentally wrong with you, rather than as specific problems which have developed for a reason, and which it might in fact be possible to resolve?

Does this sound familiar? ☐

5 Physical characteristics

You may feel that you are too tall, too short, too fat, too thin, the wrong colour, the wrong shape or the wrong build. And you might use these observations to undermine your sense of self-esteem. For instance, someone who sees themselves as overweight might feel completely fat, ugly and unattractive. They would probably ignore all the other things that made them attractive, such as their sense of style, their ability to enjoy life and their intelligence.

Does this sound familiar? ☐

6 Psychological characteristics

Psychological characteristics – especially those that have attracted criticism in childhood (such as having a high energy level or being strong-willed) – might lead you to feel bad about yourself. Instead of seeing your qualities as gifts, you might see them as further evidence that you are unacceptable to others.

Does this sound familiar? ☐

7 Differences between yourself and other people

However talented you are, there are probably other people who are more talented. However much you have, there are probably others who have more. Perhaps you use comparisons with other people as a source of evidence to support your poor opinion of yourself?

Does this sound familiar? ☐

8 Other people's behaviour towards you, past or present

People who were treated badly as children may see this treatment as evidence of their own lack of worth, whether the treatment came from family, schoolmates or the society in which they lived. Equally, dislike, rejection, disapproval or abuse in the present can be used to reinforce low self-esteem.

Does this sound familiar? ☐

9 The behaviour of others for whom you feel responsible

This is a particular trap for people with low self-esteem who become parents. They may blame themselves for anything that goes wrong in their children's lives, even long after the children have grown up and left home.

Does this sound familiar? ☐

10 Loss of something that was a part of your identity

As we said in Section 1 of this workbook, people hang their self-esteem on a range of different pegs, such as wealth, career or relationships. If the peg on which you have hung your sense of worth is taken away (for instance, if you lose your job), this may expose you to the full force of negative beliefs about yourself. It may be taken as another sign that you are not good enough, even if there are several other convincing reasons for it (e.g. the company was doing badly and had to make some cutbacks).

Does this sound familiar? ☐

How else can the 'evidence' be understood?

Each source of 'evidence' that you used to support your Old Bottom Line is open to different interpretations. Once you have identified the evidence that you feel backs up your Old Bottom Line, your next task is to examine it carefully and assess how far it truly supports what you have been in the habit of believing about yourself.

You may find the following questions useful. You will see that they relate directly to the various sources of evidence outlined above. It may also be worth bearing in mind the questions you used to tackle self-critical thoughts in Part Two.

Key Questions

When Reviewing the 'Evidence' for Your Old Bottom Line

1 Aside from personal inadequacy, what other explanations could there be for current difficulties or signs of distress?

2 Although it is useful to be able to manage independently, what might be the advantages of being able to ask for help and support?

3 How fair is it to judge yourself on the basis of past errors and failures?

4 How fair is it to judge yourself on the basis of specific shortcomings?

5 How helpful is it to let your self-esteem depend on rigid ideas about what you should do or be?

6 Just because someone is better at something than you, or has more than you do, does that make them better as a person?

7 What reasons, besides the kind of person you are, might there be for others' behaviour towards you?

8 How much power do you actually have over the behaviour of people you feel responsible for?

9 What aspects of yourself could you value and appreciate, aside from what you have lost?

1 Aside from personal inadequacy, what other explanations could there be for current difficulties or signs of distress?

If this is a time when you are having difficulties or experiencing distress, rather than taking this as a sign that there is something fundamentally wrong with you, look at what is going on in your life at the moment.

- Is anything happening that might make sense of how you are feeling?

_____

_____

_____

- If someone you cared about was going through what you are going through right now, might they feel similar?

_____

_____

_____

_____

- How would you react to them? Would you assume that they, too, must be inadequate, bad or whatever?

_____

_____

_____

_____

- Or would you consider their reactions to be understandable, given what was going on?

_____

_____

_____

_____

- Even if nothing very obvious is happening in your life right now to explain how you feel, how far could it be understood in terms of old habits of thinking which are a result of your past experiences?

_____

_____

_____

_____

2 Although it is useful to be able to manage independently, what might be the advantages of being able to ask for help and support?

You may feel that asking for help is a sign of weakness, and that you should be able to stand on your own two feet. But perhaps being able to ask for help when you genuinely need it actually puts you in a stronger position, not a weaker one, because it may give you a chance to deal successfully with a wider range of situations than you could manage on your own.

- How do you feel when other people who are in difficulties come to you for help or support?

_____

_____

_____

_____

_____

- Do you automatically conclude that they must be feeble or pathetic? If not, how do you react?

_____

_____

_____

_____

- Have you ever felt useful, wanted and warm towards another person because you were able to offer them help? Maybe this is how other people who care about you would feel about you, if you gave them half a chance?

_____

_____

_____

_____

Alternatively, you may fear that if you ask for help, you will be disappointed. Other people may refuse, or be scornful, or not be able to give you what you need. It makes sense to select people who you have no strong evidence to suppose will react in this way. That aside, the best way to test out how others will react is to try it. Work out your predictions in advance and check them out, just as you learned to do in Part Two.

3 How fair is it to judge yourself on the basis of past errors and failures?

People with low self-esteem sometimes confuse what they *do* with what they *are*. They assume that a bad action is a sign of a bad person, or that failing at something means being a failure generally. If this were true, no one in the world could ever feel good about themselves. We may regret things we have done, but it is not helpful or accurate to move on from that to complete self-condemnation.

- Do you believe that you are thoroughly bad, worthless, inadequate or useless, because of something you did in the past?

  _____

  _____

  _____

  _____

- What if, instead, you could see your past failings in terms of natural human error, or a product of your experiences?

  _____

  _____

  _____

This is not the same as letting yourself off the hook. It is a first step towards putting right whatever needs to be put right, and thinking about how you might avoid making the same mistakes in future. What you did may have been the only thing you could have done, given your state of knowledge at the time. Now you can see things differently, so you can take advantage of your broader current perspective. And remember: you may have done a bad or stupid thing, but that does not make you a bad or stupid person.

4 How fair is it to judge yourself on the basis of specific shortcomings?

Having something about yourself that you would like to improve makes you part of the human race.

- Maybe you have difficulty asserting yourself, or being punctual, or organizing your time, or talking to people without anxiety. How does it follow that there is something fundamentally wrong with you as a person?

_____

_____

_____

_____

- How would you judge another person with the same specific difficulty?

_____

_____

_____

- If your reaction to another person would be different, then what if you took a more tolerant approach to yourself?

_____

_____

_____

Remember that your shortcomings, whatever they are, are only one side of you (remember your list of positive qualities from Part Two, Section 3).

5 How helpful is it to let your self-esteem depend on rigid ideas about what you should do or be?

You may have always been aware that your self-esteem was based on a particular aspect of yourself (e.g. your ability to make people laugh, your physical strength, or your capacity to earn a high salary). Or you may have only recognized what you depended on after you had lost it (e.g. perhaps you are ageing, your physical beauty has faded, you have retired, or your family has left home).

- What does your worth depend on, *apart from* the one thing you have decided is your be-all and end-all?

_____

_____

_____

_____

- How many of the qualities, strengths, skills and talents on your list of positive qualities depend on the peg you usually hang your self-esteem on?

_____

_____

_____

_____

- Think about people you know, like and respect, and write down what attracts you to them. When you consider why you value each person, how important is the one thing your own self-esteem depends on?

_____

_____

_____

_____

_____

6 Just because someone is better at something than you, or has more than you do, does it make them better than you as a person?

The fact that some people are more beautiful, more competent, richer or more advanced in their careers does not make them any better than you as people.

- How possible is it for anyone to be best at everything?

  _____

  _____

  _____

  _____

- What might be the benefits of judging each person on their own merits?

  _____

  _____

  _____

  _____

- How would it be if you had a sense of your own worth, regardless of how you stand in relation to other people?

  _____

  _____

  _____

  _____

  _____

7 What reasons, besides the kind of person you are, might there be for others' behaviour towards you?

People with low self-esteem often assume that if others treat them badly or react to them negatively, this must in some way be deserved. This can make it difficult to set limits to what you will allow others to do to you, to feel entitled to others' time and attention, to assert your own needs, and to end relationships that damage you.

There are many possible reasons why people behave as they do. In the case of the particular person (or people) whose behaviour seems to you to back up your Old Bottom Line, ask yourself what reasons there could be?

- What, in their own early experiences, might have made it difficult for them to behave any differently (just as children who are abused or treated violently often become abusers or violent themselves)?

  _____

  _____

  _____

- What might there be, in their current circumstances, that is prompting them to behave badly (e.g. stress, pressure, illness, fear)?

  _____

  _____

  _____

- Is it possible that, without them necessarily being aware of it, you remind them of someone they do not get on with?

  _____

  _____

  _____

- Is it possible that you are simply not their cup of tea?

  _____

  _____

  _____

- How far do they behave in the same way with others? Perhaps there is nothing personal about the way they treat you – their manner is critical or sharp or dismissive with everyone, not just with you?

  _____

  _____

  _____

If you find it difficult to detach yourself from your usual self-blaming perspective and to think of other reasons why people behave towards you as they do, consider how you explain bad behaviour or unkindness towards people other than yourself. For example:

- When a case of child abuse is reported in the newspapers, who do you immediately assume is to blame – the child? Or the adult abuser?

  _____

  _____

  _____

- Similarly, if you read about intimidation, persecution, rape or assault, who do you hold responsible for that? Do you automatically conclude that the person on the receiving end must have deserved it, or can you see that the perpetrator is responsible for what he or she did?

  _____

  _____

  _____

- What about civilian victims of war? Do you consider that they are to blame for their fate, or do you see them as innocent victims of violence carried out by others for their own reasons?

  _____

  _____

  _____

In each of these cases, do you always assume that it must in some way be the fault of the person who is treated badly? Or do you explain what happened in some other way? If so, try applying similar explanations to your own experiences.

8 How much power do you actually have over the behaviour of people you feel responsible for?

It's important to remember that you have very limited power over other people's behaviour.

- For instance, if you have a dinner party, you can provide good food and drink, and you can ask a mix of people who you think will get on with one another – but how far can you guarantee that everyone will enjoy themselves?

- Likewise, how far can you prevent a teenage child from going out with friends you think are a bad influence (without forbidding your son or daughter to leave the house and completely removing the independence they need as a young adult)?

Try to be clear about the limits of your responsibility towards other people. There are some things you can realistically do to influence them (such as talking to them in a calm, caring way). But there are other things (such as what they do when they are elsewhere) that are beyond your control. It is reasonable partly to base your good opinion of yourself on your willingness to meet your responsibilities. It is not reasonable to base your self-esteem on things over which you have no control.

9 What aspects of yourself could you value and appreciate, aside from what you have lost?

- Look back at the work you did on appreciating your strong points and qualities (Part Two, Section 3). What aspects of yourself could counterbalance your sense that the peg you have hung your self-esteem on is lost?

● Think about people you like, love and respect. What is it about them that you appreciate, apart from the one thing that you have based your own self-esteem on?

_____

_____

_____

Summarizing the evidence for your Old and New Bottom Lines

Here is how Briony summarized the experiences that seemed to support her Old Bottom Line ('I am bad'), and how she now understood them after carefully thinking things through.

'Evidence' for Old Bottom Line	New Understanding
My parents died – blamed myself.	They loved me dearly and would never have left me if they could have helped it.
My step-parents' behaviour.	Not my fault – their behaviour was vicious and cruel, and there was no reason for it. No child deserves to be treated like that.
My stepfather's abuse.	It was a wicked thing to do. He knew it: that is why he concealed it. He was the adult; I was the child. He should never have abused my trust like that. It was sick.
My first marriage – husband ridiculed and criticized me, wore me down.	I now know he was like that in other relationships. Given what had already happened to me, I was in no position to fight back. My belief that I was bad made me think I deserved it.
People being irritable or unkind or putting me down.	Bound to happen sometimes – can't please everyone. Does not mean I am bad.

In the light of this new understanding, Briony now believed her Old Bottom Line: 30 per cent (as opposed to 100 per cent when she started the first workbook).

In the light of this new understanding, Briony now believed her New Bottom Line: 75 per cent (as opposed to 0 per cent).

Now (using the worksheet on pp. 93–4) complete your own summary of the experiences that have seemed to support your Old Bottom Line, and of how you now understand them.

What evidence supports your New Bottom Line?

There are two main ways of collecting new evidence that supports your New Bottom Line and contradicts the old one: observation and experiments.

Observation

Part One described how your Old Bottom Line is kept in place by negative biases in perception and interpretation. These make it easy for you to notice information that supports your Old Bottom Line, while encouraging you to screen out information that contradicts it. You worked on correcting this bias when you made your list of good points and positive qualities in Part Two, Section 3. Now you need to seek out and record information that directly contradicts your Old Bottom Line, and supports a more generous view of yourself.

The information (or evidence) you need to look for will depend on the exact nature of your Bottom Line. If, for example, your Old Bottom Line was 'I am unlikeable' and your New Bottom Line is 'I am likeable', then you will need to collect evidence that supports the idea that you are indeed likeable (for example, people smiling at you, people wanting to spend time with you, or people saying that they enjoy your company). If, on the other hand, your Old Bottom Line was 'I am incompetent' and your New Bottom Line is 'I am competent', then you will need to collect evidence that supports the idea that you are indeed competent (for example, meeting deadlines, responding sensibly to questions, or handling crises at work effectively).

In order to find out what information you personally need to look for, answer the following questions:

* What experiences (evidence) would you see as inconsistent with your Old Bottom Line?

_____

_____

_____

_____

- What information or experiences would suggest to you that your Old Bottom Line is inaccurate, unfair or invalid?

  _____

  _____

  _____

  _____

- What evidence would you see as consistent with your New Bottom Line?

  _____

  _____

  _____

  _____

- What information or experiences would suggest to you that your New Bottom Line is accurate, fair and valid?

  _____

  _____

  _____

  _____

Make sure the items on your list are absolutely clear and specific. If they are vague and poorly defined, you will have trouble deciding whether you have observed them or not.

Again, let's take Briony's summary of evidence supporting her New Bottom Line as an example.

Evidence from Briony's past is:

- My parents loved me. I know that from my own memories and from photos and things I have.

- My grandmother loved me. She couldn't protect me but she made me feel worthwhile and lovable.

- I made some friends at school, though I was too prickly and unhappy to have many (not my fault).

- Even when I was being abused in my first marriage, I managed to hold down a job, and then, after having the children, I protected them from their father. When he began to show signs of abusing them I got up the courage to leave, even though I never thought I would make it alone.

- I found a second husband who loves and supports me. He is a good man, and he chose me and stuck by me in spite of all my difficulties.

- I have struggled to overcome what happened to me, and made a good fist of it.

- All the good points on my list.

Evidence from Briony's present life is:

- Things I do for other people

- Things I contribute to society (e.g. my charity work and political activism)

- My good points, day to day (from list)

- My relationships – signs that people love me (e.g. phone calls, letters, invitations, people stopping to talk to me)

In the light of this evidence, Briony now believed her Old Bottom Line: 20 per cent

In the light of this evidence, Briony now believed her New Bottom Line: 85 per cent

Now use the worksheet on pp. 93–4 to complete your own summary of the past and present evidence that supports your New Bottom Line, and rate how far you now believe both your Old and your New Bottom Lines.

Experiments

Now is the time to push back the walls of the prison that low self-esteem has built around you, by experimenting with acting as if your New Bottom Line was true. Despite the work you have already done on rethinking your Old Bottom Line, you may still feel uncomfortable or even fearful of doing this. Notice what thoughts run through your mind when you consider entering new situations, and perhaps also when you have succeeded in being your new self and then afterwards begin to doubt how well it went. The chances are, you will find anxious predictions and self-critical thoughts behind these feelings. If so, you know how to combat them. Now fill in this section on the worksheet on pp. 93–4

Once again, the experiments you need to carry out depend on the exact nature of your New Bottom Line. Ask yourself:

- What experiences would confirm and strengthen your new perspective on yourself?

_____

_____

_____

_____

- What do you need to do in order to discover that this new perspective is useful and rings true?

_____

_____

_____

_____

- You experimented in Part Two with approaching what you usually avoided and dropping your unnecessary precautions – how does what you discovered fit here?

_____

_____

_____

_____

- What other experiments could you carry out on similar lines?

_____

_____

_____

_____

● Equally, consider the changes you made in Part Two, Section 3, when you were learning to treat yourself kindly and build rewards into your life. How do *those* fit with what you are doing now?

_____

_____

_____

_____

● Are there other similar things you could do now to strengthen your belief in your New Bottom Line?

_____

_____

_____

_____

● What would someone who believed your New Bottom Line do, on a day to day basis?

_____

_____

_____

_____

For example, to strengthen her 'I am worthy' Bottom Line, Briony decided to improve her social life by:

● Making the first approach to people she trusted, rather than waiting for them to contact her

● Gradually being more open about herself with people

● Planning treats and pleasures for herself

Make a list of as many experiments as you can think of in different areas of life, under the following headings:

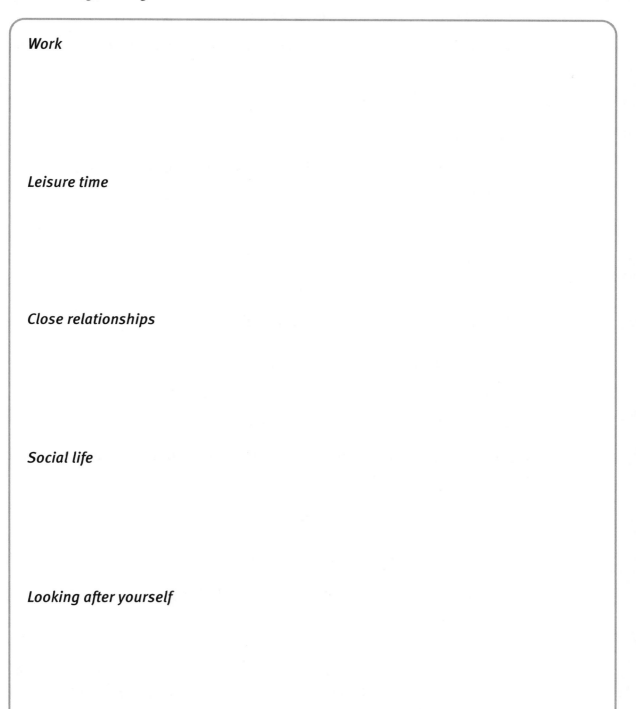

Work

Leisure time

Close relationships

Social life

Looking after yourself

Here are some more examples, to give you some ideas:

If you are usually a perfectionist about your work, try…

- Dropping your standards and spending less time preparing reports and documents
- Going for 'good enough'

If you usually worry about your weight, try…

- Wearing brightly coloured, stylish clothes instead of trying to fade into the wallpaper
- Eating something you enjoy, with relish

If you usually rehearse everything before you say it, try…

- Saying the first thing that comes into your head
- Showing what you really feel about something

If you are usually apologetic about asking people for anything, try…

- Acting as if you were entitled to time and attention
- Asking for help even when you don't really need it

If you usually agree to do things for other people in order to get their approval, try…

- Saying 'no'
- Doing something just for yourself

If you usually avoid talking about your feelings, try…

- Asking a friend for help when something upsets you
- Showing someone how much you like them

When you have a list of specific experiments, covering all these aspects of your life, transfer them to the worksheet on p. 94 which summarizes your work on your Bottom Line. And then begin to put them into practice in your daily life.

Here is Briony's summary, as an example:

Observation: Information and experiences I need to be alert to, in order to gather more evidence to support my New Bottom Line

- Things I do for other people, especially all the time and care I put into the children. My love for them, and for my husband. The pleasure I take in them. My creativity and imagination in looking after them and helping them to develop into good people.

- Things I contribute to society (my charity work, my political activism).

- My good points as they show themselves day to day.

- My relationships – signs that people love me – phone calls, letters, invitations, people stopping to talk to me and wanting me to get involved in things.

- My intelligence – at last I am starting to think I am worth educating, and doing something about it.

Experiments: Specific things I need to do, in order to gather more evidence to support my New Bottom Line

- Begin making the first approach to people I trust, rather than leaving it up to them.

- Gradually be more open about myself with people, and see if they really do back off.

- Plan treats and pleasures for myself – I deserve it.

- Make time to study. Start saving for a proper course.

- Give more responsibility to the others at home to keep the show on the road.

- Look for a better job, one that really uses what I have got to offer.

Assessing the outcome of your experiments

Make sure that you assess the outcome of your experiments carefully, just as you assessed the outcome of your experiments when you checked out your anxious predictions in Part Two. Keeping a careful record of your observations and your experiments, and of exactly what you did and how it turned out, will allow you to accumulate information to support your New Bottom Line. You will find worksheets to help you do this on pp. 90–2. There is also a blank worksheet, which you can photocopy if you wish, on p. 126.

90

Acting in Accordance with my New Bottom Line

Date/Time	Experiment (what I did)	Results (what I noticed, my feelings and thoughts, others' reactions, what I learned)	My belief in my Old Bottom Line	My belief in my New Bottom Line

Acting in Accordance with my New Bottom Line

Date/Time	Experiment (what I did)	Results (what I noticed, my feelings and thoughts, others' reactions, what I learned)	My belief in my Old Bottom Line	My belief in my New Bottom Line

Acting in Accordance with my New Bottom Line

Date/Time	Experiment (what I did)	Results (what I noticed, my feelings and thoughts, others' reactions, what I learned)	My belief in my Old Bottom Line	My belief in my New Bottom Line

Undermining Your Bottom Line: Summary Sheet

When you have rated your degree of belief, take a moment to focus on your Bottom Line and notice what feelings emerge. Write down any emotions you experience (e.g. sadness, anger, guilt), and rate them according to how powerful they are (from 0 to 100). Again, you may notice that, although you can still call up your Bottom Line, your feelings when you focus on it are less intense.

My Old Bottom Line is: 'I am _____ **,**

	Belief	Emotions (0–100)
When the Old Bottom Line is most convincing:	____ %	
When it is least convincing:	____ %	
When I started the book:	____ %	

My New Bottom Line is: 'I am _____ **,**

	Belief	Emotions (0–100)
When the New Bottom Line is most convincing:	____ %	
When it is least convincing:	____ %	
When I started the book:	____ %	

'Evidence' supporting the Old Bottom Line and how I now understand it:

'Evidence'   **New Understanding**

With my new understanding, I now believe my Old Bottom Line: ____ %

With my new new understanding, I now believe my New Bottom Line: ____ %

Evidence (past and present) which supports my New Bottom Line:

_____

_____

_____

_____

_____

In the light of this evidence, I now believe my Old Bottom Line: _____%

In the light of this evidence, I now believe my New Bottom Line: _____%

Observation: Information and experiences I need to be alert to, in order to gather more evidence to support my New Bottom Line:

_____

_____

_____

_____

_____

_____

Experiments: Specific things I need to do, in order to gather more evidence to support my New Bottom Line:

_____

_____

_____

_____

_____

Creating and strengthening a New Bottom Line does not happen overnight. It may take weeks (or even months) of observation and experimentation before you find your New Bottom Line fully convincing. You have accumulated a lifetime of evidence that supports your Old Bottom Line. So you should expect to make some investment in time and energy, some regular commitment to record-keeping and practice, in order to reach the point where thinking and acting in accordance with your New Bottom Line becomes second nature.

Summary

1 The final step towards overcoming low self-esteem is to identify your Bottom Line in your own words. There are a number of different sources of information you can use to do this.

2 Once you have identified your old, negative Bottom Line, you can move on right away to formulate a more positive, balanced alternative. This will help you to begin noticing information you have previously screened out, which contradicts your old beliefs about yourself.

3 The next step is to identify the evidence you have used to support your Old Bottom Line, and to examine whether you can find other ways of understanding it – instead of assuming that it reflects your real self.

4 Your final task is to decide what experiences and information would support your New Bottom Line and to begin to seek them out, both through observation and by experimenting with acting as if your New Bottom Line was true and observing the results.

SECTION 3: Planning for the Future

This section will show you ways of making sure that the changes you have made are consolidated and carried forward, rather than left behind when you close the last workbook.

Old habits die hard. Particularly at times when you are stressed, or when you are feeling low or unwell, your Old Bottom Line may surface again, and – along with it – your old habits of expecting the worst and criticizing yourself may begin to re-establish themselves.

There is no need to worry about this. You now know how to break the vicious circle that keeps low self-esteem going, and you have established new Rules for Living and a New Bottom Line. It will simply be a question of going back to what you already know and putting it into practice again until you have got yourself back on an even keel. If you are aware that a setback could occur, you will be in a good position to spot early warning signs that your Old Bottom Line is resurfacing and to deal with it without delay. You may be able to put it back in its place almost immediately, or it may take you a little time.

Either way, you will have an opportunity to discover again that the new ideas and skills you have acquired can work for you. By planning ahead and considering how setbacks might come about, you will ensure that the changes you have made will last in the long term.

This section will help you to:

- update your understanding of your low self-esteem
- draft an Action Plan for the future, using Key Questions and SMART criteria
- fine-tune your Action Plan so that it has the best chance of being helpful to you

Updating your understanding of your low self-esteem

The flowchart on p. 100 explains the development and persistence of low self-esteem. You are already familiar with this, from Parts One and Two. You will see that here we have used the flowchart to summarize the different methods you have learned to use as you have made your way through the workbooks, both to undermine your Old Bottom Line and to establish and strengthen your New Bottom Line. This is so that you can see clearly how the changes you have made fit together in a coherent plan for overcoming low self-esteem.

Opposite the flowcharts on pp. 100 and 102, you will find blank versions with just the headings, and space left for you to write. Here is your opportunity to review and update the work you did earlier (in Part One, Sections 2 and 3), when you charted a personal picture of the development and persistence of your low self-esteem. You may find that the picture now is much the same, or you may find that working on your anxious and self-critical thoughts, on enhancing self-acceptance, and on creating new Rules for Living and a New Bottom Line, has helped you to understand more fully the story of your low self-esteem. Use the flowcharts to summarize your up-to-date understanding of how the problem came into being, and what kept it going.

Drafting an Action Plan

The point of an Action Plan is to have something which you can easily review and refer to when you need it, for example to check your progress or to remind you how to manage a setback. This means that:

- **It must be easy to find**. If you cannot find your Action Plan, you will not be able to make use of it. And leaving it lying around to get stained and dog-eared is like sending a message to yourself that it doesn't really matter. So make sure that you look after your Action Plan. You need to know where it is, and be able to find it easily when you need to. Decide right now where you want to keep it. Put it somewhere special, if you can: somewhere that is yours and yours alone.

- **It must be short**. Your Action Plan will be most helpful to you if it is not too long. If there are points you want to go into in more detail, put them on separate sheets and staple them to the Action Plan worksheets in this workbook. And if there are particular parts of any of the workbooks that you want to be able to come back to easily, get some coloured Post-It notes and stick them in the books so that these parts are easy to identify.

Your Action Plan – The first draft

In pencil, so that it is easy to change and improve, write down your answers to the questions you will find on pp. 107–9, using the worksheets on pp. 110–17. Also make a note of any other helpful points that occur to you as you follow the questions through. This is the first draft of your Action Plan.

When you have completed your first draft, review it and see if you have left out anything important. Go back through all three workbooks, including what you have written on the charts and worksheets, to remind yourself of everything you have done. When you are satisfied that you have the best possible version for the time being, put your Action Plan into practice for two or three weeks.

Your Action Plan – The second draft

After two or three weeks of putting your first draft into practice, you should have a good idea of how helpful your Action Plan is. Now is a good time to review it and refine it, if you wish. You may find that you have left out something vital, or that what seemed clear to you when you wrote it down seems less helpful when you try to apply it in real life.

Make whatever changes seem necessary, and then write out a revised version for a longer test-drive. Decide for yourself how long you will practise applying this version – perhaps three months? Or six months? This will give you an opportunity to find out how helpful the plan is in the longer term, how well-established your New Bottom Line is, and how consistently it influences how you feel about yourself in everyday life. You also need to get an idea of how well your Action Plan helps you to deal with the times when your old Bottom Line resurfaces.

Your Action Plan – The final draft

After a longer period of practice, review your Action Plan once again:

- How helpful has it been to you?

- How well did it keep you on track?

- Has it enabled you to continue to grow and develop?

- Has it helped you deal with setbacks in the best possible way?

If all is well, your second draft may be your final draft. If, on the other hand, your Action Plan still has shortcomings, you will need to make whatever changes are necessary, test-drive your new version for a limited period, and then review it again. When you are happy with it, write it out in pen.

Remember that, unless you have superhuman powers to foretell the future, your Action Plan will never cover everything. However helpful it is, you should still be prepared to change and fine-tune it at any point in the future when you realize it could be extended or improved.

Undermining the Negative Beliefs that Lie at the Heart of Low Self-Esteem

(Early) Experience
What experiences (events, relationships, living conditions) contributed to the developments of your negative beliefs about yourself?

What experiences contributed to keeping them going?

Are these experiences part of the 'evidence' that supports your low opinion of yourself?

↓

The Bottom Line
On the basis of experience, what conclusions did you draw about yourself? What were your old, negative beliefs about yourself?

What perspective on yourself would make better sense? What is your New Bottom Line?

What 'evidence' did you use to support your New Bottom Line? How else could you understand this 'evidence'?

↓

What experiences (evidence) support your New Bottom Line and contradict the old one?

What new information (things you have screened out/discounted) do you need to be alert to?

What experiments do you need to carry out?

↓

Changing Unhelpful Rules:

Rules for Living
What are your Rules for Living? In what ways are they unreasonable and unhelpful?
What alternatives would be more reasonable and helpful?
How can you test-drive them?

Undermining the Negative Beliefs that Lie at the Heart of Low Self-Esteem

(Early) Experience

↓

The Bottom Line

↓

↓

Changing Unhelpful Rules:

Rules for Living

Breaking the Vicious Circle

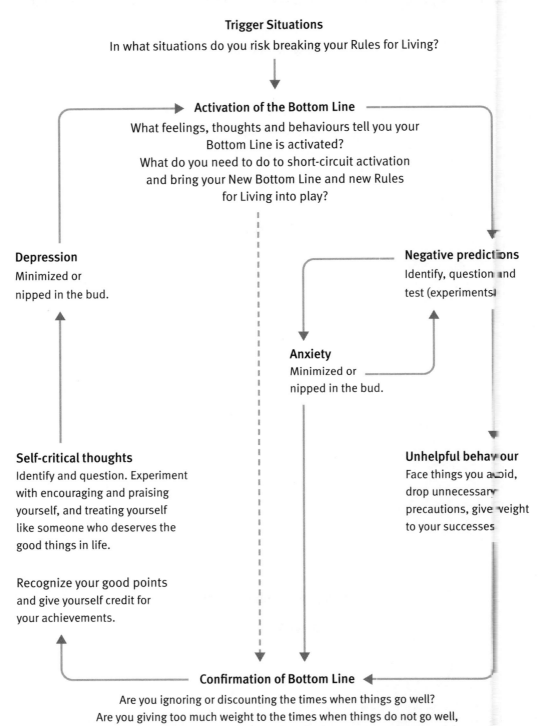

Trigger Situations

In what situations do you risk breaking your Rules for Living?

Activation of the Bottom Line

What feelings, thoughts and behaviours tell you your
Bottom Line is activated?
What do you need to do to short-circuit activation
and bring your New Bottom Line and new Rules
for Living into play?

Depression

Minimized or
nipped in the bud.

Negative predictions

Identify, question and
test (experiments)

Anxiety

Minimized or
nipped in the bud.

Self-critical thoughts

Identify and question. Experiment
with encouraging and praising
yourself, and treating yourself
like someone who deserves the
good things in life.

Recognize your good points
and give yourself credit for
your achievements.

Unhelpful behaviour

Face things you avoid,
drop unnecessary
precautions, give weight
to your successes

Confirmation of Bottom Line

Are you ignoring or discounting the times when things go well?
Are you giving too much weight to the times when things do not go well,
and assuming they say something about you as a person?

Breaking the Vicious Circle

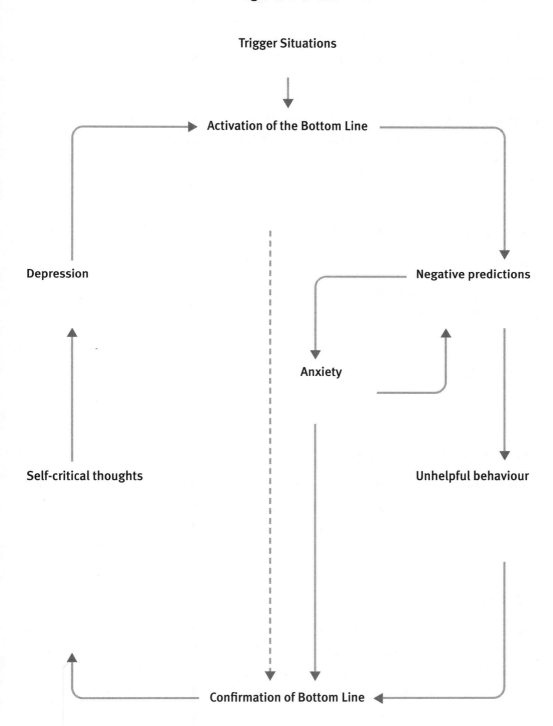

Trigger Situations

Activation of the Bottom Line

Depression

Negative predictions

Anxiety

Self-critical thoughts

Unhelpful behaviour

Confirmation of Bottom Line

Fine-tuning your Action Plan: Getting SMART

Whichever stage you are at – first, second or final draft – make sure that your Action Plan meets the following **SMART** criteria. If your plan is not crystal clear, you may find after a few weeks that you are no longer certain what you are supposed to be doing. If your plan is too ambitious, you will not be able to carry it out successfully, and that could be demoralizing. If on the other hand it is too limited, you may feel that you have stopped making progress. The **SMART** criteria will help you to ensure that your Action Plan takes you where you want to go.

Action Planning: SMART Criteria

Is it SMART?

Is it: **S**imple and **S**pecific enough?
Is it: **M**easurable?
Is it: **A**greed?
Is it: **R**ealistic?
Is the: **T**imescale reasonable?

S: Is it Simple and Specific enough?

Can you explain what you plan to do in words of one syllable? Is it so straightforward that even a child could understand it? To check this, try reading it out to a trusted friend or a member of your family. If they ask you to explain or clarify any of it, that part needs redrafting. When you have redrafted it, check out how it sounds to them.

M: Is it Measurable?

How will you know when you have achieved what you set out to do? For example, in six months' time, if you have successfully acted on your Action Plan, how will you be feeling? Which of your new habits will still be in place? What specific targets will you have reached? How will you know that your New Bottom Line is still going strong?

If you can specify clearly what you are going for, it will be much easier for you to judge how successfully you are putting it into practice, and to assess how helpful it is to you.

A: Is it Agreed?

Changes in you will mean changes for other people. For example, if you are planning to become more assertive about getting your needs met, then this will inevitably have an impact on those around you. If you are planning to change how you organize your working life (e.g. to reduce your working hours, in order to have more leisure time), then again this will have an impact on other people, both at work and at home.

When you make your Action Plan, it is important to take this into account. Do you need to communicate your intentions to others? Would it help to negotiate some of the changes you want with your family or friends? What about asking for help in sticking to your plan?

Even if you do not wish to involve others directly, consider what impact changes in you will have on them. Are they likely to react negatively in any way? What do you predict? You could, of course, be wrong – but you will be in a stronger position to stay on course if you have considered realistically what might happen, and planned how you will deal with it (if necessary, with outside support).

Part of Briony's plan, for example, was to give herself more time to do things she enjoyed. She realized that she had allowed her family to get used to leaving all the housework to her. She decided that it would be a good idea to tell them about the work she had been doing to improve her self-esteem, and that she planned to start a fairer system of sharing the housework. She predicted that her family would see the justice of this, in theory, and would be in favour of what she was trying to do. She also predicted that, in practice, they would be reluctant to do their bit and would prefer to leave things as they were. So, in her plan, she included careful details of what to do when her family failed to change along with her. This included reminding herself of her reasons for making the change: she was a worthy person who deserved more out of life than to be a skivvy.

R: Is it Realistic?

When you plan ahead, take into account:

- Your state of emotional and physical health and fitness
- Your resources (e.g. money, time, people who care about and respect you)
- Other demands on your time and energy
- The level of support you have from friends, family, colleagues and others

Your Action Plan will be most solid and realistic if it takes these factors into account.

T: Is the Timescale reasonable?

Finally, make sure that you have considered carefully how much time you are willing to devote to putting your Action Plan into practice, and what timescale seems reasonable in order to achieve whatever targets you have set yourself. This may well include deciding what changes are most important to you, and which are less of a priority.

Ask yourself:

- What are your priorities? If you could complete only 20 per cent of your plan, which 20 per cent would you want it to be?

- If you believe it would still be helpful for you to write down and question your thoughts regularly, how much time will you need to set aside every day for this?

- How much time might you need every week (or month) to assess how things are going and to set yourself new challenges?

- What are your personal objectives, as far as self-esteem is concerned? Where do you want to be after three months? After six months? After one year?

- How frequently will you review your progress (successes, difficulties, what helped you, and what got in your way)?

- Have you set a date for your first review? This could be next week, or next month, or further away. Whenever it is, decide on a definite date and make an appointment with yourself. Make your review a special occasion. Take yourself out for lunch or give yourself a day out in the country, or at a health spa. At the very least, find a peaceful space in your house, and choose a time when you will not be interrupted, so that you can reflect on what you have achieved and think ahead.

Write down the date and time of your review in your diary or on your calendar right now. And do not allow yourself to put it off. This is something you are doing for yourself. It is important. And you deserve it.

When drawing up your Action Plan ask yourself the Key Questions in the box on the next page.

Key Questions

When Drawing up an Action Plan

1 How did my low self-esteem develop?

2 What kept it going?

3 What have I learned from these workbooks?

4 What were my most important unhelpful thoughts, rules and beliefs? What alternatives did I find to them?

5 How can I build on what I have learned?

6 What might lead to a setback for me?

7 If I do have a setback, what will I do about it?

Let's take Briony's Action Plan for the Future as an example, using these key questions.

1 How did my low self-esteem develop?

When my parents died, I felt it was my fault. When my step-parents treated me so badly, that confirmed it. Finally, when my stepfather began to abuse me, I came to the conclusion that everything that had happened was a result of something in me. It all meant I was BAD. This was my Old Bottom Line. Once this idea was in place, other things happened that seemed to confirm it. For example, my first marriage was to a man who constantly criticized and ridiculed me. Because of what had happened earlier on, I thought this was just what I deserved.

2 What kept it going?

I kept on acting and thinking as if I really was a bad person. I never paid attention to good things about myself. I kept my true self hidden from people, because I was convinced that if they found out what I was really like, they would want nothing further to do with me. I was always very hard on myself. Anything I got wrong filled me with despair – yet more evidence of what a bad person I was. I could not have close relationships, except with the few people who persisted even when I held back. I allowed people to dismiss me and treat me badly. I didn't think I deserved anything better.

3 What have I learned from these workbooks?

To understand things better – it's my *belief* that I'm bad that's the problem, not that I really am bad. I have learned that it is possible to change beliefs about yourself that have been around for a long time, if you work on them. I have learned to still my critical voice and focus on the good things about me. I am changing my rules and taking the risk of letting people see more of the true me.

4 What were my most important unhelpful thoughts, rules and beliefs? What alternatives did I find to them?

Unhelpful thought/rule/belief	*Alternative*
I am bad _____	I am worthy _____
If I let anyone get close to me, they will hurt and exploit me. I must never allow anyone to see my true self.	If I let people get close to me, I get the warmth and affection I need. Most people will treat me decently and I can protect myself from those who don't. Since my true self is worthy, I need not hide it. If some people don't like it, that's their problem.

5 How can I build on what I have learned?

Read the summary sheets for my new rules and Bottom Line daily – I need to drum them in. Keep acting as if they were true and observe the results. When I notice myself getting anxious and wanting to avoid things or protect myself, work out what I am predicting and check it out. Watch out for self-criticism – it is deeply entrenched and I need to keep fighting it. Keep on recording examples of good things about me – it has already made a difference. Make time for me – don't be afraid to remind the family when they go back to their old ways.

6 What might lead to a setback for me?

Getting depressed for any reason. Being consistently badly treated by someone. Something going very wrong for someone I cared about (I would tend to blame myself).

7 If I do have a setback, what will I do about it?

Try to notice the early warning signals, for a start. Ask my husband to help with this – he's sensitive to when I start hiding myself away and being irritable and defensive, and he notices when I start being down on myself. Then get out my notes, especially the Summary Sheets and this Action Plan, and follow through on what I know works. Don't be hard on myself for taking a backward step – it's bound to happen from time to time, given how long I have felt bad about myself and how I came to be that way. Be encouraging and kind to myself, get all the support I can, and go back to the basics.

Now use the worksheet on pp. 110–17 to draw up your own **Action Plan for the Future.**

My Action Plan for the Future

1 How did my low self-esteem develop?

Briefly summarize the experiences that led to the formation of your Old Bottom Line. Also include later experiences that have reinforced it, if they are relevant.

2 What kept it going?

Briefly summarize your old unhelpful Rules for Living, and the thinking that fuelled your vicious circle (your anxious predictions and self-critical thoughts). What did you automatically screen out, ignore or discount? Finally, note the unnecessary precautions and self-defeating behaviour that prevented you from discovering that your predictions were not accurate and conspired to keep you down.

3 What have I learned from these workbooks?

Make a note of the new ideas you have found most helpful (e.g. 'My beliefs about myself are opinions, not facts'). Also include particular methods you have learned for dealing with anxious and self-critical thoughts, rules and beliefs (e.g. 'Review the evidence and look at the bigger picture'). Look back over what you have done and make a note of whatever you personally found most useful in practice.

4 What were my most important unhelpful thoughts, rules and beliefs? What alternatives did I find to them?

Write down the anxious predictions, self-critical thoughts, Rules for Living and Bottom Lines that caused you most trouble. Against each one, summarize the alternative you have discovered.

Unhelpful thought/rule/belief	Alternative

My Action Plan continues

5   How can I build on what I have learned?

Here is your opportunity to consider in detail what you need to do, in order to ensure that the new ideas and skills you have learned become a routine part of your life. It is also your chance to work out what changes you still want to make. This may include going back to particular parts of these workbooks and going through some sections again. It might also include further reading, or deciding to seek help in order to take what you have discovered further or put it into practice more effectively (see pp. 119–22).

Ask yourself:

- Are there aspects of how your low self-esteem developed and what kept it going that you do not yet understand fully (Part One)? If so, how could you clarify them?

- Are there still situations where you feel anxious (Part Two, Section 1) but you are not clear why? Or situations where you understand very well what your anxious predictions are, but you have not yet faced them fully without dropping all your unnecessary precautions? If so, how will you use what you have learned to tackle these situations, and to deal with future anxieties?

- How will you ensure that you continue to spot and challenge self-critical thoughts (Part Two, Section 2)? What self-defeating behaviours do you still need to watch out for? What do you plan to do instead?

- How good are you at keeping your good points in mind and noticing examples of your qualities, strengths, skills and talents (Part Two, Section 3)? Do you still need to keep a written record? Even if you do not, might it not be a useful resource to look over, if you have a setback at some point in the future?

- When you look at the pattern of your day and your week, are you achieving a good balance between 'M' activities (duties, obligations, tasks) and 'P' activities (pleasure, relaxation)? If so, how will you ensure that you continue to do so? And if not, then how can you build on the changes you have already made?

My Action Plan continues

- Are you routinely giving yourself credit for what you do and appreciating your achievements? If so, how can you ensure that you continue to do so? If not, why not – and what do you need to do about it?

- How convincing do you now find your new Rules for Living (Part Three Section 1)? What do you still need to do (if anything) to strengthen their credibility and make acting on them second nature? What experiments do you need to carry out? What thoughts are getting in your way, and how can you tackle them?

- How far are you now able to act as if your New Bottom Line was true? If you believe your New Bottom Line strongly and act routinely as if it was true, how can you ensure that it stays rock solid, even at times of pressure or distress?

6 What might lead to a setback for me?

Consider what experiences or changes in your circumstances might still activate your Old Bottom Line. For example, supposing you were experiencing a high level of stress, or your life circumstances had become very difficult, or you were tired or unwell or upset for some other reason, this might still make you vulnerable to self-doubt. Working out what your own personal vulnerabilities might be will prepare you to notice quickly when things go wrong and do something about it.

7 How do I know if I'm having a setback?

The first, crucial thing is to notice what is happening. What cues would tell you that your Old Bottom Line was back in operation?

- How would you expect to feel?

- What might be going on in your body?

My Action Plan continues

- What thoughts and images might run through your mind?

- What might you notice about your own behaviour (e.g. beginning to avoid challenges, dropping pleasurable activities, not standing up for yourself any more)?

- What might you notice in others (e.g. irritation, reassurance, apologies)?

8 If I notice my old Bottom Line coming back into operation, what will I do?

The next thing is to consider in detail what to do if you spot the beginnings of a setback. How can you nip it in the bud?

Firstly, **DON'T PANIC!** It is quite natural to have setbacks on your journey towards overcoming low self-esteem, especially if the problem has been with you for a long time. Setbacks do not mean that you are back to square one, or that there is no point in doing anything further to help yourself. On the contrary, you simply need to return to what you have learned and begin putting it into practice regularly, until you have got yourself back on an even keel. This may mean going back to basics (e.g. starting to write things down regularly again, perhaps after you have stopped needing to do so for some time). This is not a backward step. It is simply a sensible recognition that, for a limited period, you need to put in some extra time and effort to strengthen your New Bottom Line.

Summary

1 The ideas and techniques you have learned from these workbooks form a complete programme for change.

2 To ensure that you carry forward what you have learned and make it part of your life, it is important to make a written Action Plan for the future.

3 Your Action Plan should be straightforward and realistic. Make sure that you can measure your progress in carrying it out, and that it takes into account the impact of changes in you on those around you. It should also take account of limitations in your time and resources, and the timescale should be realistic.

4 In your Action Plan, summarize your understanding of how your low self-esteem developed and what kept it going. Note what you have learned as you worked your way through this course, and how you plan to build on your new ideas and skills. Identify future events and stresses that might lead to setbacks for you, and work out what to do if one occurs.

5 Well done for completing the course! This is a real achievement – and you are taking away valuable tools to cope with the challenges and setbacks you may face in the future.

Useful Books and Addresses

Useful Books

Alberti, Robert E. and Emmons, Michael L., *Your Perfect Right: A Guide to Assertive Living*, Impact Publishers, 1994

Beck, Aaron T., *Love is Never Enough*, Penguin Books, 1989

Burns, David D., *Feeling Good: The New Mood Therapy*, Avon Books, 1999

Burns, David D., *The Feeling Good Handbook*, Penguin, 2000

Butler, Gillian, *Overcoming Shyness and Social Anxiety*, Robinson, 1999

Butler, Gillian and Hope, Tony, *Manage Your Mind: The Mental Fitness Guide*, Oxford University Press, 1995

Gilbert, Paul, *Overcoming Depression*, Robinson, 1997

Glouberman, Dina, *Life Choices, Life Changes: Develop your Personal Vision with Imagework*, Hodder & Stoughton, 2003

Greenberger, Dennis and Padesky, Christine A., *Mind Over Mood: Cognitive Treatment Therapy Manual for Clients*, Guilford Press, 1995

Lerner, Harriet, G., *The Dance of Anger: A Woman's Guide to Changing the Pattern of Intimate Relationships*, HarperCollins, 1999

McKay, Matthew and Fanning, Patrick, *Prisoners of Belief: Exposing and Changing Beliefs That Control Your Life*, New Harbinger Publications, 1991

Young, Jeffrey and Klosko, Jan, *Reinventing Your Life: How to Break Free From Negative Life Patterns*, Penguin Putnam, 1994

Useful addresses

Academy of Cognitive Therapy
One Belmont Avenue, Suite 700
Bala Cynwyd, PA 19004
USA
Tel / Fax: (001) 610 664 1273 / 610 664 5137
Email: info@academyofct.org

British Association for Behavioural and Cognitive Psychotherapies
The Globe Centre
PO Box 9
Accrington BB5 0XB
Tel / Fax: 01254 875277 / 01275 239114
Email: babcp@babcp.com
Website: www.babcp.org.uk

(They have a list of cognitive behavioural therapists accredited by the organization)

British Association for Counselling and Psychotherapy
BACP House
35–37 Albert Street
Rugby
Warwickshire CV21 2SJ
Tel / Fax: 0870 443 5252 / 0870 443 5161
Website: www.bacp.org.uk

British Psychological Society
St Andrew's House
48 Princess Road East
Leicester LE1 7DR
Tel / Fax: 0116 254 9568 / 0116 247 0787
Email: mail@bps.org.uk
Website: www.bps.org.uk

(They hold a directory of chartered clinical psychologists, the people most likely in this country to be trained in cognitive behaviour therapy)

Center for Cognitive Therapy
Po Box 5308
Huntington Beach, CA 92615-5308
USA
Tel / Fax: (001) 714 963 0528 / 714 963 0538
Email: mooney@padesky.com
Website (for health professionals): www.padesky.com
Website (for members of the public): www.mindovermood.com

Center for Cognitive Therapy
5435 College Avenue
Oakland, CA 94618
USA
Tel / Fax: (001) 510 652 4455 / 510 652 3872
Website: www.sfbacct.com

Cognitive Therapy Center of New York
120 E 56th Street
New York, NY
USA
Tel: (001) 212 221 0700
Website: www.schematherapy.com

International Association of Cognitive Psychotherapy
Department of Psychology, Box 5025
University of Southern Mississippi
Hattiesburg, MS 39406-5025
USA
Tel / Fax: (001) 601 266 4602 / 601 266 5580
Website: www.cognitivetherapyassociation.org

MIND: The National Association for Mental Health
Granta House
15–19 Broadway
Stratford
London E15 4BQ
Infoline: 0845 766 0163
Website: www.mind.org.uk

Newcastle Cognitive and Behavioural Therapies Centre
Plummer Course
Carliol Place
Newcastle-upon-Tyne NE1 6UR
Tel / Fax: 0191 219 6288 / 0191 219 6282

No Panic
93 Brands Farm Way
Telford TF3 2JQ
Helpline (Freephone): 0808 808 0545
Website: www.nopanic.org.uk

Oxford Cognitive Therapy Centre
Department of Clinical Psychology
Warneford Hospital
Oxford OX3 7JX
Tel: 01865 223986
Email: octc@oxmhc-tr.nhs.uk
Website: www.octc.co.uk

Extra Charts and Worksheets

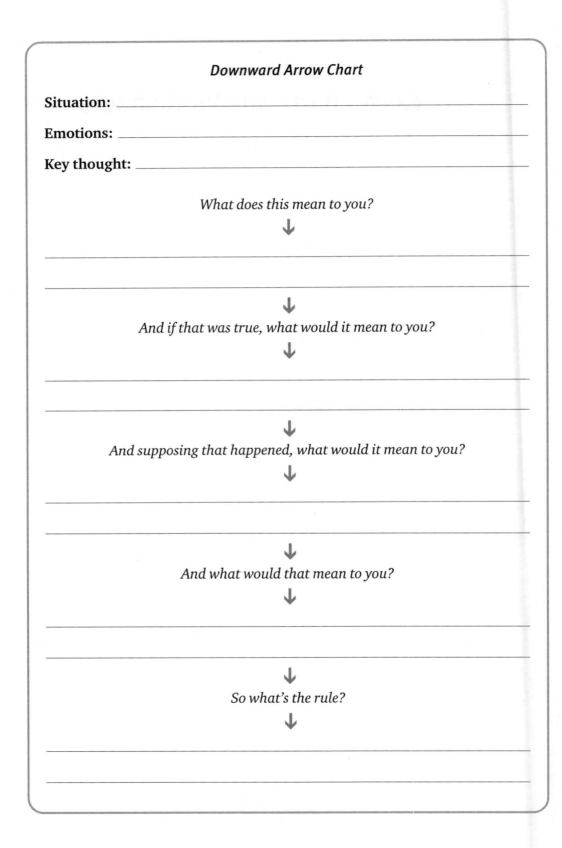

Downward Arrow Chart

Situation: _____

Emotions: _____

Key thought: _____

What does this mean to you?

↓

_____

_____

↓

And if that was true, what would it mean to you?

↓

_____

_____

↓

And supposing that happened, what would it mean to you?

↓

_____

_____

↓

And what would that mean to you?

↓

_____

_____

↓

So what's the rule?

↓

_____

_____

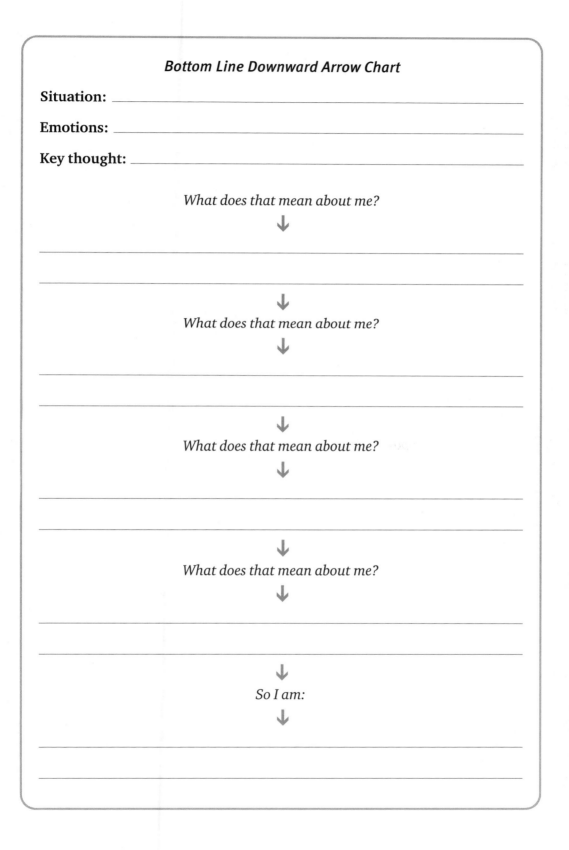

Bottom Line Downward Arrow Chart

Situation: _____

Emotions: _____

Key thought: _____

What does that mean about me?

↓

_____

_____

↓

What does that mean about me?

↓

_____

_____

↓

What does that mean about me?

↓

_____

_____

↓

What does that mean about me?

↓

_____

_____

↓

So I am:

↓

_____

_____

Acting in Accordance with my New Bottom Line

Date/Time	Experiment (what I did)	Results (what I noticed, my feelings and thoughts, others' reactions, what I learned)	My belief in my Old Bottom Line	My belief in my New Bottom Line

Undermining the Negative Beliefs that Lie at the Heart of Low Self-Esteem

(Early) Experience

↓

The Bottom Line

↓

↓

Changing Unhelpful Rules:

Rules for Living

Breaking the Vicious Circle

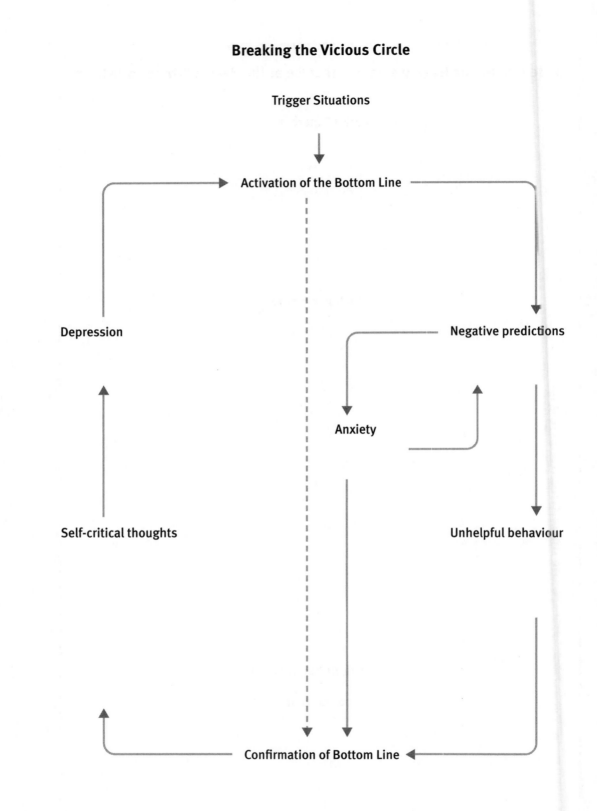

Trigger Situations

Activation of the Bottom Line

Depression

Negative predictions

Anxiety

Self-critical thoughts

Unhelpful behaviour

Confirmation of Bottom Line

Experimenting with New Rules Worksheet

Date/time	The situation	What I did	The outcome (what I noticed, felt, thought, learned)

Thoughts and Reflections

Thoughts and Reflections

Thoughts and Reflections